QUICK & EASY *Crochet*

QUICK & EASY *Crochet*

FAST AND STYLISH PATTERNS FOR SCARVES, TOPS, BLANKETS, BAGS, AND MORE

Melody Griffiths

CICO BOOKS
LONDON NEW YORK

This edition published in 2024 by CICO Books
an imprint of Ryland Peters & Small Ltd
341 E 116th St, New York, NY 10029

www.rylandpeters.com

10 9 8 7 6 5 4 3 2 1

First published in 2007 as *Crochet in No Time*.

Text © Melody Griffiths 2024
Design, illustration, and photography © CICO Books 2024

**The designs in this book are copyright and must not
be crocheted for sale.**

ISBN: 978 1 80065 334 4

Printed in China

Editor: Marie Clayton
Designer: Alison Fenton
Photographers: Tino Tedaldi, Debbie Patterson,
and Geoff Dann
Stylist: Sue Rowlands
Illustrator: Stephen Dew

In-house editor: Jenny Dye
Art director: Sally Powell
Creative director: Leslie Harrington
Head of production: Patricia Harrington
Publishing manager: Carmel Edmonds

MIX
Paper from
responsible sources
FSC® C106563

Contents

Chapter 4
Babies & Children 70

Chapter 5
Equipment & Techniques 106

Introduction

With this stunning collection of 35 things to make, you have the choice of creating items for your home, for yourself, or for your family and friends. My mother taught me to crochet when I was about five years old. I can still remember how easy it was to make the stitches and how exciting it was to see the work grow. I've since extended my knowledge and experience as a hand-knit designer to creating garments using those basic crochet stitches learned so long ago.

Crochet is so simple and so versatile. All you need to get started is a hook and some yarn. The action of catching and looping the yarn soon builds up into stitches, making crochet one of the fastest ways of creating a fabric. And the feel of the fabric can vary enormously, depending on the combination of hook size, yarn type, and stitch pattern; crochet can be firm, floppy, lacy, textured, soft, crisp, flat, or three-dimensional.

With these designs, I've tried to find new ways of exploring and exploiting simple crochet stitches and techniques. Sometimes this means breaking the rules and substituting a single crochet and two chain for the more usual three turning chain to give a neater edge, or choosing a fancy fashion yarn rather than the classic smooth yarns usually associated with crochet. And wherever possible, I've tried to make the stitch patterns simpler to do—for instance, working into spaces rather than into chain to make it easier to see where to place the hook for fine lacework or when working with heavily textured yarns.

If you've never tried crochet before, the techniques section will provide you with everything you need to know to get started. And the nicest thing about crochet is that once you've grasped the basics, you can make anything. Each project indicates the time it took to crochet the item, as well as tips to help you decide if a project is right for you and your lifestyle.

There are projects worked in the round, projects worked in rows, projects that took less than an hour to make, scrap-yarn projects, heirloom projects, projects for beginners, and projects that require more determination. There are unusual motifs and original ideas—everything from simple scarves and wraps to toys, shapely garments, lacy trims, and heirloom baby clothes. With so many to choose from, you're sure to find some that are irresistible.

Enjoy creating with crochet!

Chapter 1
Scarves, Hats & Accessories

Pansy Motif Scarf

This pretty scarf is a scrap-yarn project. The naturalistic effect of the pansy motif is enhanced by working it in shades of purple and pink with a flash of yellow at the center. Different height stitches make lifelike petals, with chain gaps in the last round to flute the edges and give a convenient place to join the motifs. The rows of pansies are sewn on a simple mesh scarf that's really quick to work.

ESTIMATED TIME TO COMPLETE

Each pansy took 20 minutes; complete scarf, 9 hours.

YARN

Debbie Bliss Cashmerino DK (55% merino wool, 33% acrylic) light worsted (DK) weight yarn, approx. 120yd (110m) per 1¾oz (50g) ball
- 1 ball in Buttercup 09 (yellow) (A)
- 1 ball in each of Black 03 and Claret 25 (dark purple) (B)
- 1 ball in each of Lilac 21, Blackberry 19 (purple), and Rose 23 (pink) (C)
- 2 balls in Sea Green 81 (D)

HOOK AND EQUIPMENT

E/4 (3.50mm) crochet hook
Yarn needle

FINISHED MEASUREMENTS

Width 6¼in (16cm); **length** 48in (122cm)

GAUGE

Each pansy motif measures 2½in (6.5cm) wide and 2¾in (7cm) high, 5 spaces and 8 rows to 4in (10cm) over mesh patt, when pressed, using E/4 (3.50mm) hook. Change hook size if necessary to obtain this size motif and this gauge.

ABBREVIATIONS

ch = chain; **cont** = continue; **dc** = double crochet; **dtr** = double treble; **hdc** = half double crochet; **RS** = right side; **sc** = single crochet; **sp(s)** = spaces; **ss** = slip stitch; **tr** = treble; **WS** = wrong side; **[ ]** = work instructions in brackets as directed

TIPS

- Yarn amounts are approximate and may vary according to the brand and fiber content of the light worsted (DK) yarn you use.
- To work the long sc stitches, insert the hook in 2ch sp of first round as directed and pull the loop up to the height of the 4th round, tension the strands to lie flat on the motif between the two dc stitches of the 2nd round, then complete the sc.
- Changing the colors you use for A, B, and C adds to the flowery effect.
- Finish your motifs quickly and neatly by working over the ends and snipping them off; then you'll only need to darn in the last end.
- Different brands of light worsted yarn may be slightly different in thickness, so the size of the pansy motifs could vary slightly.
- If you prefer, instead of joining the pansies in rows, just scatter them at random all over the scarf.

PANSY MOTIF

Using A, make 4ch, ss in first ch to form a ring. Cont in A.

Round 1 (RS) 1ch, [1sc, 2ch] 6 times in ring, ss in first sc. Fasten off. Join B in a 2ch sp.

Round 2 (RS) 1ch, 1sc in same sp as join, [2ch, 2sc in next sp] 5 times, 2ch, 1sc in first sp, ss in first sc.

Round 3 Ss in next sp, [1ch, 1hdc, ss] in same sp as first ss, [ss, 3ch, 4dc, 3ch, ss] in each of next 2 sps, [ss, 1hdc, ss] in foll sp, [ss, 1ch, 3sc, 1ch, ss] in each of next 2 sps, ss in first sp. Fasten off.
Join C to the right of the first large petal.

Round 4 1ch, inserting hook in 2ch sp of first round below, work 1 long sc, continue working behind petals made on 2nd and 3rd rounds, [5ch, 1 long sc in next sp of first round] twice, 3ch, [1 long sc in next sp of first round, 4ch] twice, 1 long sc in last sp of first round, 3ch, ss in first sc.

Round 5 [1sc, 1hdc, 1dc, 1ch, 1dc, 3tr, 1ch, 3tr, 1dc, 1ch, 1dc, 1hdc, 1sc] in each 5ch sp, [1sc, 1dc, 1ch, 1dc, ss] in 3ch sp, [ss, 1hdc, 1dc, 1ch, 3dc, 1ch, 1dc, 1hdc, ss] in each 4ch sp, [ss, 1dc, 1ch, 1dc, 1sc] in 3ch sp, ss in first sc. Fasten off.

Make 18 motifs, joining in rows of 3 by working 1sc instead of 1ch in corresponding 1ch sp of large and small petals.

SCARF

First side Using D, make 34ch.

Row 1 (RS) 1sc in 2nd ch from hook, [6ch, miss 3ch, 1sc in next ch] 8 times.

Row 2 8ch, 1sc in first 6ch sp, [6ch, 1sc in next 6ch sp] 7 times, 3ch, 1dtr in last sc.

Row 3 1sc in dtr, [6ch, 1sc in next 6ch sp] 7 times, 6ch, 1sc in 5th ch.
Rows 2 and 3 form the mesh pattern.
Work 43 more rows. Fasten off.

2nd side Work as first side, do not fasten off.

Joining row With WS together and 2nd side facing, work 1sc in 5th ch of first side, [4ch, 1sc in next 6ch sp of both sides together] 7 times, 4ch, 1sc in 5th ch of 2nd side and dtr of first side together. Fasten off. Weave in ends (see page 119).

TO FINISH

Press scarf to open out the mesh. With short ends of scarf level with center of first row of pansies, sew three rows of three pansies on each end of the scarf.

Black Lace Purse

The bold, lacy pattern for the side panels is worked in rows using just chain, double crochet, and treble crochet, with the occasional longer stitch. The pattern is arranged on the half drop, so you quickly get accustomed to the repeat. The silk lining panels are stiffened with fusible web, then the lacy side panels are stretched over them, giving the purse a boxy shape.

ESTIMATED TIME TO COMPLETE

The purse took 6 hours.

YARN AND MATERIALS

DMC Natura Just Cotton (100% cotton) fingering (4-ply) weight yarn, approx. 170yd (155m) per 1¾oz (50g) ball
  2 balls in Noir (11)

20 x 22in (50 x 56cm) piece of red silk dupion

22 x 10in (56 x 25cm) piece of ultrahold fusible web

Magnetic purse catch

Black and red sewing thread

33½in (84cm) length of plastic-coated wire

HOOK AND EQUIPMENT

C/2 (2.50mm) crochet hook

Hand-sewing needle

Yarn needle

FINISHED MEASUREMENTS

Width (at top edge) 9½in (24cm); **height** 8¼in (21cm)

GAUGE

One repeat measures 2½in (6cm) across, 8 rows to 2¾in (7cm), when pressed using a C/2 (2.50mm) hook. Change hook size if necessary to obtain this gauge.

ABBREVIATIONS

ch = chain; **cont** = continue; **dc** = double crochet; **foll** = following; **rep** = repeat; **RS** = right side; **sc** = single crochet; **ss** = slip stitch; **st(s)** = stitch(es); **tr** = treble; [ ] = work instructions in brackets as directed.

TIPS

- When pressing the side panels, spray lightly with a little aerosol starch so they keep their shape when using them as templates for the lining.

- For accurate curves along the scalloped lower edge, make a pattern by drawing around the side panel on graph paper. This will make it easy to check that each scallop is the same.

- If you prefer, leave out the magnetic catch and insert a zipper in the top edge of the lining.

SIDE PANELS

(Make 2)
Make 50ch.
Row 1 (RS) 1sc in 2nd ch from hook, [1sc in each ch] to end. 49 sts.
Row 2 1ch, 1sc in first sc, 1sc in each of next 2sc, [* 4ch, miss 3sc, 1dc in next sc, 4ch, miss 3sc *, 1sc in each of next 5sc] 3 times, rep from * to *, 1sc in each of last 3sc.
Row 3 1ch, 1sc in first sc, 1sc in next sc, [* 3ch, 4dc in next 4ch sp, 1ch, 4dc in foll 4ch sp, 3ch *, miss 1sc, 1sc in each of next 3sc] 3 times, rep from * to *, miss 1sc, 1sc in each of last 2sc.
Row 4 1sc in first sc, 5ch, [4dc in next 3ch sp, 3ch, 1tr in 1ch sp, 3ch, 4dc in foll 3ch sp, 3ch, miss 1sc, 1dc in next sc, 3ch] 4 times, omitting last 3ch.
Row 5 1sc in first dc, 2ch, [4dc in next 3ch sp, 3ch, 1sc in foll 3ch sp, 1sc in tr, 1sc in next 3ch sp, 3ch, 4dc in foll 3ch sp, 1ch] 4 times, omitting last ch, 1dc in 2nd ch.

Row 6 1sc in first dc, 2ch, 1dc in same dc as sc, [* 4ch, 1sc in next 3ch sp, 1sc in each of next 3sc, 1sc in foll 3ch sp, 4ch *, 4dc in 1ch sp] 3 times, rep from * to *, 2dc in 2nd ch.
Row 7 1sc in first dc, 2ch, [4dc in next 4ch sp, 3ch, miss 1sc, 1sc in each of next 3sc, 3ch, 4dc in next 4ch sp, 1ch] 4 times, omitting last ch, 1dc in 2nd ch.
Row 8 1sc in first dc, 6ch, [* 4dc in next 3ch sp, 3ch, 1dc in center sc, 3ch, 4dc in foll 3ch sp, 3ch *, 1tr in 1ch sp, 3ch] 3 times, rep from * to *, 1tr in 2nd ch.
Row 9 1ch, 1sc in tr, 1sc in first 3ch sp, [* 3ch, 4dc in next 3ch sp, 1ch, 4dc in foll 3ch sp, 3ch, 1sc in next 3ch sp *, 1sc in tr, 1sc in foll 3ch sp] 3 times, rep from * to *, 1sc in 3rd ch.
Row 10 1ch, 1sc in first sc, 1sc in next sc, 1sc in first 3ch sp, [* 4ch, 4dc in 1ch sp, 4ch, 1sc in next 3ch sp*, 1sc in each of next 3sc, 1sc in foll 3ch sp] 3 times, rep from * to *, 1sc in each of last 2sc.
Work Rows 3 to 10 again, then Rows 3 to 9.
Last row 1ch, 1sc in first sc, 1sc in next sc, [* 4sc in 3ch sp, 1sc in each of next 4dc, 1sc in 1ch sp, 1sc in each of foll 4dc, 4sc in 3ch sp *, 1sc in each of next 3sc] 3 times, rep from * to *, 1sc in each of last 2sc.
Fasten off.

HANDLES

(Make 2) Make 5ch, ss in first ch to form a ring. Work 7sc in ring. Cont in sc working in a spiral until handle measures 16in (40cm). Fasten off.

LINING

Press side panels. Fold silk in half, place starting chain edge (top) of one side panel on fold and use as a template to cut 2 double pieces of silk lining with a ½in (1cm) seam allowance at sides and lower edge. Cut fusible web to exact size of side panels. Open out folded lining and fuse web to WS of each piece, from fold line to lower edge. Remove backing paper from web. Put one half of the purse catch onto the web, just below the fold line on each side and centered. Fold the other half of the lining over the catch and fuse in place over the entire area, working carefully around the catch. Make a tiny rolled hem along the raw edges. Repeat for the other lining panel.

GUSSET

With RS of one side panel facing, join yarn to top left starting ch.
Row 1 Work 44sc down left side edge, 1sc in each of 81sc along lower edge and 44sc up right side edge. *(169 sts.)*
Row 2 1ch, [1sc around stem of each sc] to end.
Row 3 1ch, [1sc in each sc] to end.
Cont in sc, work 2 more rows.
Fasten off.
Work 2nd side to match; do not fasten off.

TO FINISH

Sew edges of linings to side panels. Return to 2nd side of gusset, with RS facing and working through one stitch from each side each time, join last row of each side of gusset with sc. Fasten off and weave in ends (see page 119). Cut plastic-coated wire in half, turn wire up at each end, and insert one piece in each handle. Sew handles on purse.

Shaded Fluted Scarf

Increasing along one edge makes a deep frill that automatically curls around to give a soft fluted effect. The scarf is worked in double crochet on a chain and single crochet base.

ESTIMATED TIME TO COMPLETE

The scarf took 6½ hours.

YARN

Rowan Kidsilk Haze (70% mohair, 30% silk) lace (2-ply) weight yarn, approx. 230yd (210m) per ¾oz (25g) ball
  1 ball in each of
  Liqueur 595 (A)
  Candy Girl 606 (B)
  Grace 580 (C)

HOOK AND EQUIPMENT

I/9 (5.50mm) crochet hook

Yarn needle

FINISHED MEASUREMENTS

Width 3½in (8cm); **length** (along shorter edge) 56¼in (143cm)

GAUGE

13 sts in single crochet and 6 rows in patt to 3⅛in (8cm) using I/9 (5.50mm) hook. Change hook size if necessary to obtain this gauge.

ABBREVIATIONS

ch = chain; **dc** = double crochet; **foll** = following; **patt** = pattern; **sc** = single crochet; **st(s)** = stitch(es); **[ ]** = work instructions in brackets as directed.

NOTE

The hook size given is larger than would usually be used with this yarn to give a very soft, open fabric.

TIP

▓ If you want to make the scarf all in one color, you'll need just two balls of Rowan Kidsilk Haze yarn.

SCARF

Using A, make 198ch.

Row 1 1sc in 2nd ch from hook, [1sc in each ch] to end. *(197 sts.)*

Row 2 1sc in first sc, 2ch, [1dc in each sc] to end.

Row 3 1sc in first dc, 2ch, [2dc in next dc, 1dc in foll dc] to last 2 sts, 2dc in next dc, 1dc in 2nd ch. *(295 sts.)* Change to B.

Row 4 1sc in first dc, 2ch, [2dc in each of next 2dc, 1dc in foll dc] to last 3 sts, 2dc in each of next 2dc, 1dc in 2nd ch. *(491 sts.)*

Row 5 1sc in first dc, 2ch, [2dc in each of next 4dc, 1dc in foll dc] to end, placing last dc in 2nd ch. *(883 sts.)* Change to C.

Row 6 1sc in first dc, [1dc in next dc, 2dc in each of next 6dc, 1dc in each of foll 2dc] to end, placing last dc in 2nd ch. *(1471 sts.)*

Fasten off. Weave in ends (see page 119).

String Tote

Made entirely from ordinary string, this boxy little tote is created with just four flat pieces of single crochet. The knotted decoration and handles are easy to do; they're worked using flat knots, which are simply square knots tied around a core.

ESTIMATED TIME TO COMPLETE

It took 5 hours to crochet the tote, plus 2 hours to make up and add decoration.

YARN

Natural cream-colored thin 100% cotton parcel string with a glazed finish, slightly thicker than a light worsted (DK) yarn, with approximately 109yd (100m) to 3oz (84g)

408yd (375m) in cream

Thick cotton parcel string, similar to worsted (Aran) yarn, though denser, with approximately 66yd (60m) to 3oz (84g)

66yd (60m) in natural

HOOK AND EQUIPMENT

E/4 (3.50mm) crochet hook

Blunt-pointed needle

FINISHED MEASUREMENTS

Width 10in (25.5cm); **length** 9½in (24cm)

GAUGE

15 sts and 18 rows to 4in (10cm) over single crochet using E/4 (3.50mm) hook. Change hook size if necessary to obtain this gauge.

ABBREVIATIONS

ch = chain; **sc** = single crochet;
[ ] = work instructions in brackets as directed.

NOTES

Buy a large spool of thin string, even if it is more than you need, so you'll have fewer ends to darn in. If you use small balls of string, join in at the start of a row so the ends can be hidden in the edging.

Amounts given are approximate because string can vary.

If you want a plain tote, you won't need the contrast string. Omit the knotted decoration and add braided or crochet handles.

TIPS

■ To decorate your tote with flowers instead of knots, crochet motifs from the Irish Lace Pillow on page 64, or from the Rosebud Hairband on page 72 and sew them on.

BACK AND FRONT

Using the thinner string, make 41ch.
Row 1 1sc in 2nd ch from hook, [1sc in each ch] to end. *(40 sc.)*
Row 2 1ch, [1sc in each sc] to end. Row 2 forms single crochet. Work 42 more rows sc. Fasten off.
Work 2nd piece in the same way.

SIDE PANELS

Panel 1 Make 7ch.
Work Row 1 as given for back and front. *(6sc.)*
Work 63 rows sc. Fasten off.
Panel 2 Work as Panel 1 but do not fasten off. Join last row of Panel 1 to last row of Panel 2 with sc. Fasten off.

EDGING

Placing chain edge of back and front at top, matching rows at sides and rows to stitches along lower edge, insert hook one stitch in from edge each time to join back and front to side panels with a row of sc. Fasten off and weave in ends (see page 119).

KNOTTED DECORATION

Using the thicker string, cut 4 lengths, each 2¾yd (2.5m) long. Fold 2 lengths in half and loop through on Row 11 down from top edge of front between 19th and 20th stitches, fold and loop through remaining 2 lengths between 21st and 22nd stitches, making 2 groups of 4 strands.

First flat knot Leaving a loop at top right, take the first 2 strands on the right over in front of the center 4 strands and under the last 2 strands on the left, then take these last 2 strands on the left behind the center 4 strands and out through the loop of 2 strands on the right. Pull ends gently to tighten first half of knot. The outer strands have changed places. Leaving a loop out to the left, take the last 2 strands on the left over in front of the center 4 strands and under the last 2 strands on the right, then take these last 2 strands on the right behind the center 4 strands and out through the loop of 2 strands on the left. Pull ends to tighten completed knot. Work another flat knot using the same strands.

2nd line of knots Cut 4 more slightly shorter lengths of string and loop 2 through between 17th and 18th stitches, and 2 between 23rd and 24th stitches, 14 rows down from top edge. Use 4 strands from center and 4 new strands to work 2 flat knots at each side.

3rd, 4th, and 5th lines of knots Using slightly shorter lengths of string for each group of 4 strands and spacing the new strands 3 rows down and 2 stitches out each time, join in and work 2 flat knots 3 times on 3rd line, 4 times on 4th line, and 5 times on 5th line.

6th, 7th, 8th, 9th lines of knots Leaving 4 strands at each side each time, work 2 flat knots 4 times on 6th line, 3 times on 7th line, twice on 8th line, and once on 9th line. Thread each group of 4 strands through between adjacent stitches to hold the last 4 lines of knots flat on the front of the tote. To finish each group of ends in a tassel, fold two of the ends and loop them through again to make 6 shorter lengths. Wrap the two longer

ends around close to the tote, knot to secure, then thread a blunt-pointed needle with the ends to take them back through the tote, out again, and down through the wrapping. When all tassels have been made, trim ends.

HANDLES

For each handle Cut 6 lengths of thicker string for the core, each 39½in (100cm) long. Cut 4 lengths of thin string, each 2¾yd (2.5m) long. Line up ends of both strings and tie in a firm overhand knot about 3¼in (8cm) from the end. Use the thinner string to cover the core with flat knots, ending with an overhand knot 3¼in (8cm) from end. Sew handles on each side of tote. Trim ends.

Scarf with Pockets

Super bulky yarn and simple stitches on a huge hook make this a quick-to-finish project. Tuck your hands into the patch pockets or use them to hold small items.

ESTIMATED TIME TO COMPLETE

The scarf took 2 hours.

YARN

Rowan Big Wool (100% merino wool) super bulky (super chunky) weight yarn, approx. 97yd (80m) per 3½oz (100g) ball
3 balls in Reseda 69 (green) (A)
1 ball in Pantomime 79 (pink) (B)

HOOK AND EQUIPMENT

P/16 (12.00mm) crochet hook
Yarn needle

FINISHED MEASUREMENTS

Width 8¼in (21cm); **length** 65½in (166.5cm)

GAUGE

6 sts and 8 rows to 4in (10cm) over single crochet using P/16 (12.00mm) hook. Change hook size if necessary to obtain this gauge.

ABBREVIATIONS

ch = chain; **cont** = continue; **RS** = right side; **sc** = single crochet; **st(s)** = stitch(es); **WS** = wrong side; **[ ]** = work instructions in brackets as directed.

TIPS

- Work the starting chain very loosely. Each chain loop should be almost ⅞in (2cm) long.
- When working the last row of sc, tension the loop at the top of each stitch to match the starting chain.
- The pockets in the picture are left open at the top. If you prefer, you could leave them open at the sides.
- For an even quicker and simpler scarf, simply leave off the pockets.

SCARF

Using A, make 101ch.
Row 1 (WS) Working into back loop each time, 1sc in 2nd ch from hook, [1sc in each ch] to end. *(100 sts.)*
Row 2 1ch, [1sc in each sc] to end.
The 2nd row forms single crochet.
Cont in sc, work 15 more rows.
Fasten off.
Pockets (Make 2) Using B, make 9ch.
Work first row as given for scarf. *(8 sts.)*
Work 9 rows sc. Fasten off. Darn in ends.

TO FINISH

Press according to ball band. Pin pockets in place on RS at each end of scarf. Using A, work surface chain around three sides of each pocket. Sew pocket edges under surface chain and remove pins.

Simple Shell Scarf

All you need to know for the one-row pattern used for this beautiful scarf is how to do chain and double crochet. The pretty stitch has rows of shells with spaces between, so it's easy to see exactly where you are in the pattern, and because each row measures almost an inch, it grows quickly too.

ESTIMATED TIME TO COMPLETE

Each row of shell pattern took about 3 minutes. The scarf took 6 hours.

YARN

Debbie Bliss Cashmerino Aran (55% merino wool, 33% acrylic, 12% cashmere) worsted (Aran) weight yarn, approx. 98yd (90m) per 1¾oz (50g) ball
   5 balls in Ruby 610

HOOK AND EQUIPMENT

H/8 (5.00mm) crochet hook

Yarn needle

FINISHED MEASUREMENTS

Width 5½in (14cm); length 79in (200cm)

GAUGE

Four shell patts measure 5½in (14cm), 7 rows to 4in (10cm) over shell patt using H/8 (5.00mm) hook. Change hook size if necessary to obtain these gauges.

ABBREVIATIONS

ch = chain; patt(s) = pattern(s); sc = single crochet; [ ] = work instructions in brackets as directed.

TIPS

■ The scarf is worked in two halves from the center so that the shell pattern will run in the same direction on both sides when the ends of the scarf hang down.

■ Make the starting chain loosely; if necessary, use a larger size hook.

■ There is no right or wrong side to the pattern, which makes the scarf fully reversible.

■ The scarf takes just over two balls for each half, so you could make it longer if you prefer. If you want to count the rows, there should be 70 rows in each half.

■ If you prefer a wider scarf, add six chains for each extra shell and repeat the instructions in square brackets one more time for each extra shell. If you make the scarf wider, remember to buy extra yarn or your scarf won't be as long as in the pictures.

SCARF

First half Make 27ch.

Row 1 5dc in 6th ch from hook, [miss 2ch, 1dc in next ch, miss 2ch, 5dc in next ch] 3 times, miss 2ch, 1dc in last ch.

Row 2 3ch, miss first dc, [miss next 2dc, 5dc in next dc, miss next 2dc, 1dc in next dc] 4 times, working last dc in top ch.

The 2nd row forms the shell patt. Work until the scarf measures 39½in (100cm) from starting chain. Fasten off.

Second half Join yarn in first ch of first row. Working into chain on first row, complete as first half. Fasten off. Weave in ends (see page 119).

Cloche Hat with Flower

This pretty hat is just double crochet worked in rounds from the top down. There are five increase rounds; then you carry on straight. Weave in the ends, roll up the brim, and it's ready to wear. The yarn is bulky, so it works up quickly but is soft with a pearly sheen that makes the stitches show up beautifully. The flower uses single crochet, half double crochet, and double crochet, and is so simple you'll want to make more than one!

ESTIMATED TIME TO COMPLETE

The hat took 1 hour and 20 minutes, plus 15 minutes for the flower.
Total time taken, 1 hour 40 minutes.

YARN

Debbie Bliss Super Chunky Merino (100% merino wool) super bulky (super chunky) weight yarn, approx. 87yd (80m) per 3½oz (100g) ball
    2 balls in Ecru 01
    1 ball in Teal 09 (optional, if you would like to make the flower in a different color)

HOOK

K/10½ (7.00mm) crochet hook

FINISHED MEASUREMENTS

Circumference 22in (55.5cm);
flower 4¼in (11cm)

GAUGE

9 sts and 5 rows to 4in (10cm) over double crochet using K/10½ (7.00mm) hook. Change hook size if necessary to obtain this gauge.

ABBREVIATIONS

ch = chain stitch; **dc** = double crochet; **foll** = following; **hdc** = half double crochet; **sc** = single crochet; **sp** = space; **ss** = slip stitch; **st(s)** = stitch(es); **[ ]** = work instructions in brackets as directed.

HAT

Wind yarn around finger to form a ring.
Round 1 3ch, 9dc in ring, pull end to close ring, ss in 3rd ch. *(10 sts.)*
Round 2 3ch, 1dc in same place as ss, [2dc in each dc] to end, ss in 3rd ch. *(20 sts.)*
Round 3 3ch, 1dc in same place as ss, [1dc in next dc, 2dc in foll dc] 9 times, 1dc in next dc, ss in 3rd ch. *(30 sts.)*
Round 4 3ch, 1dc in same place as ss, [1dc in each of next 2dc, 2dc in foll dc] 9 times, 1dc in each of next 2dc, ss in 3rd ch. *(40 sts.)*
Round 5 3ch, 1dc in same place as ss, [1dc in each of next 3dc, 2dc in foll dc] 9 times, 1dc in each of next 3dc, ss in 3rd ch. *(50 sts.)*
Round 6 3ch, [1dc in each dc] to end, ss in 3rd ch.
The 6th round forms double crochet.
Cont in dc, work 10 more rounds.
Fasten off.
Weave in ends (see page 119) and roll up brim.

FLOWER

Wind yarn around finger to make a ring.
Round 1 1ch, 12sc in ring, pull end to close ring, ss in first sc. 12 sts.
Round 2 1sc in same place as ss, [3ch, miss 1sc, 1sc in next sc] 5 times, 3ch, miss 1sc, ss in first sc.
Round 3 [1sc, 1hdc, 1dc, 1hdc, 1sc] in each 3ch sp.
Round 4 Taking hook behind, ss around first sc of 2nd round, [5ch, ss around next sc of 2nd round] 5 times, 5ch, ss in first ss.
Round 5 [1sc, 1hdc, 3dc, 1hdc, 1sc] in each 5ch sp, ss in first dc.
Fasten off.
Weave in ends and sew on side of hat.

TIPS

▨ When working double crochet in rounds, you will get a neater join if you work the first and second chains at the start of the round tightly and the third quite loosely. This will make it easier to slip the hook under both loops of the 3rd chain to work the step stitch at the end of the round.

▨ Sew a pin on the back of the flower and use it as a corsage.

Victorian-style Collar

This airy, authentic-looking lace collar has been designed to be as easy as possible to make. It begins with a picot row because it's easier to work into and between picots than to count fine chain. The motifs and the edging pattern use the simplest stitches, and the pattern is organized to work into spaces, not chain, to make it easy on the eye despite the fineness of the lace.

ESTIMATED TIME TO COMPLETE
Each motif took 15 minutes, collar 7½ hours.

YARN
20-count (equivalent to 2ply) crochet cotton (100% cotton), 436yd (400m) per 1¾oz (50g) ball
    1 ball in white

HOOK AND EQUIPMENT
No. 12 steel (0.75mm) crochet hook

Yarn needle

Spray starch or spray sizing

FINISHED MEASUREMENT
Around neck edge (adjustable) 21½in (55cm)

GAUGE
6 picots on first row, and 11 spaces on 2nd row measure 2in (5cm) along shorter edge of neckband, and each motif measures 1¼in (4.5cm) across, all when pressed, using No. 12 steel (0.75mm) hook. Change hook size if necessary to obtain this size motif.

ABBREVIATIONS
ch = chain; **dc** = double crochet; **2dctog** = leaving last loop of each stitch on the hook, work two dc, yo and pull through 3 loops on hook; **3dctog** = leaving last loop of each stitch on hook, work 3 dc, yoh and pull through 4 loops on hook; **rep** = repeat; **RS** = right side; **sp(s)** = space(s); **ss** = slip stitch; **st(s)** = stitch(es); **sc** = single crochet; **yoh** = yarn over hook; **[ ]** = work instructions in brackets as directed.

NOTES
You can adjust the collar to fit around a smaller or larger neckline. Work more or fewer picot loops on the first row to of the neckband to fit around the neckline of your garment and adjust the 2nd row to a multiple of 11 spaces. Make one motif for each 11 spaces to join along the band on the first row of the edging. For a heavier weight cotton, adjust the hook size to obtain a fabric that feels right, then adjust the length of the neckband as described above.

TIPS
- For a neat finish, don't make an extra chain when fastening off; just snip the thread and pull it through the last stitch to give a softer, smoother line, then weave the end in thoroughly.

- For a decorative effect make motifs and sew them on a plain garment, scattered at random or in a row.

NECKBAND
Row 1 5ch, 1dc in first ch, [6ch, 1dc in 5th ch from hook] 54 times. *(55 picots.)*
Work along straight edge.
Row 2 (RS) 5ch, 1dc in first picot sp, [2ch, 1dc over ch between picots, 2ch 1dc in next picot sp] to last picot sp, 2ch, 1dc in first ch. *(110 sps.)*
Row 3 1ch,1sc in first dc, [5ch, 1sc] in each sp to end, working last sc in 3rd ch. Fasten off.

MOTIF
Make 8ch, ss in first ch to form a ring.
Round 1 (RS) 1ch, [1sc in ring, 4ch] 7 times, 1sc in ring, 2ch, 1dc in first sc.
Round 2 3ch, 2dctog in dc sp, [4ch, 3dctog in next sp] 7 times, 2ch, 1dc in 2dctog.
Round 3 3ch, 2dctog in dc sp, [4ch, 3dctog] twice in each of next 7 sps, 4ch, 3dctog in first sp, 2ch, 1dc in 2dctog.
Round 4 1ch, 1sc in dc sp, [5ch, 1sc in next sp] 15 times, 5ch, ss in first sc. Fasten off.
Make 9 more motifs.

EDGING
Lay motifs out in a row. With RS facing, join thread in first sp of Row 3 of neckband.

Row 1 (RS) 1ch, 1sc in same sp as join, * [7ch, 1sc in next sp of neckband] 3 times, 3ch, 1sc in first sp of 1st motif, 3ch, 1sc in next sp of neckband, [1ch, 1sc in next sp of 1st motif, 1ch, 1sc in next sp of neckband] twice, 3ch, 1sc in next sp of 1st motif, 3ch, 1sc in next sp of neckband, [7ch, 1sc in next sp of neckband] 3 times **, 2ch, 1sc in next sp of neckband, rep from * 8 more times to join next 8 motifs, then rep from * to ** to join 10th motif, working 4ch, 1dc in last sp of neckband instead of last 7ch, 1sc in next sp.

Row 2 1ch, 1sc in first sp, 2ch, 2dctog in same sp, [1ch, 3dctog in next 7ch sp] twice, * 1ch, [3dctog in next 5ch sp, 7ch] 11 times, 3dctog in foll 5ch sp **, [1ch, 3dctog in next 7ch sp] 6 times, rep from * 8 more times, then rep from * to **, [1ch, 3dctog in 7ch sp] 3 times.

Row 3 * 3ch, ** 1sc in next 7ch sp, 3ch, [3dctog, 3ch] 3 times in foll 7ch sp, rep from ** 4 more times, 1sc in next 7ch sp, 3ch, 1sc in center 1ch sp, rep from * 9 more times, ending last rep 1sc in last 2dctog.

Row 4 3ch, *1dc in each of next 2 sps, [5ch, 1dc in next sp] twice, 5ch, rep from * 3 more times, 1dc in each of next 2 sps, ** 5ch, 1dc in foll sp, 5ch, 1dc in each of next 6 sps, 5ch, 1dc in next sp, 5ch, 1dc in each of next 2 sps, *** [5ch, 1dc in next sp] twice, 5ch, 1dc in each of next 2 sps, rep from *** two more times, then rep from ** 8 more times, [5ch, 1dc in next sp] 3 times, 1dc in foll sp, 3ch, 1sc in same sp as 3dctog. Fasten off.
Turn and join yarn at base of first picot at neck edge.

Row 5 1ch, [1sc, 5ch, ss in sc, 1sc] in each of first 4 sps, [1sc, 5ch, ss in sc, 1sc] twice in each 5ch sp, [1sc, 5ch, ss in sc, 1sc] in each of last 4 sps, ss in base of picot.
Fasten off.

TO FINISH
Weave in ends (see page 119).
Starch the collar, place RS down on a pressing board, pat into shape, pin out each picot, and press.
Leave to dry before removing pins.

Beaded Beret

This beautiful beret is both effective and very simple to make. It's worked in rows using different height stitches to shape the segments. Adding the beads to outline the segments is easy; just thread them on and bring them up close between the stitches on a single crochet row.

ESTIMATED TIME TO COMPLETE

3½ hours, including threading the beads.

YARN AND MATERIALS

Debbie Bliss Cashmerino Chunky (55% wool, 33% acrylic, 12% cashmere) bulky (chunky) weight yarn, approx. 71yd (65m) per 1¾oz (50g) ball

   3 balls in Pearl 23 (pale pink)

492 medium size glass beads

HOOK AND EQUIPMENT

G/6 (4.50mm) crochet hook

Yarn needle

FINISHED MEASUREMENTS

To fit average-sized head
Circumference: 19in (48cm)

GAUGE

Each segment measures 2¼in (5.5cm) at widest part, 1¼in (3cm) at brim edge, 13 rows to 4in (10cm) using G/6 (4.50mm) hook. Change hook size if necessary to obtain this gauge.

ABBREVIATIONS

ch = chain stitch; **hdc** = half double crochet; **RS** = right side; **sc** = single crochet; **2sctog** = insert hook in first stitch and pull loop through, insert hook in 2nd stitch and pull loop through, yarn over hook and pull through 3 loops on hook; **ss** = slip stitch; **st(s)** = stitch(es); **dc** = double crochet; **[ ]** = work instructions in brackets as directed.

NOTES

Thread 203 beads on each of two balls of yarn and 58 beads on the third ball. Use beaded yarn for the segments and yarn without beads for top and brim edging. The beads hang between stitches, so they are not included in stitch counts.

BERET

First segment Make 30ch.

Row 1 (RS) Bring a bead up close to the hook, 1sc in 2nd ch from hook, [bring a bead up close to hook, 1sc in next ch] to end. *(29 sts.)*

Row 2 1ch, 1sc in each of first 5sc, 1hdc in each of next 3sc, 1dc in each of next 9sc, 1hdc in each of next 6sc, 1sc in each of next 3sc, ss in next sc, turn and leave 2sc.

Row 3 Ss in ss, 1sc in each of next 3sc, 1hdc in each of next 6hdc, 1dc in each of next 9dc, 1hdc in each of next 3hdc, 1sc in each of next 5sc.

Row 4 1ch, 1sc in each of next 5sc, 1hdc in each of next 3hdc, 1dc in each of next 9dc, 1hdc in each of next 6hdc, 1sc in each of next 6 sts.

Row 5 1ch, [bring bead up close to hook, 1sc in next st] to end.
Rows 2 to 5 form the pattern.

2nd to 15th segments Pattern 56 rows.

16th segment Work 2nd, 3rd and 4th rows.
Fasten off.

Close top Join back seam. With RS facing, join yarn at seam.

Round 1 Work 1sc in each segment, ss in first sc. *(16 sts.)*

Round 2 1ch, [2sctog] 8 times, ss in first st. *(8 sts.)*

Round 3 1ch, [2sctog] 4 times, ss in first st. *(4 sts.)*
Fasten off.

Brim edging With RS facing, join yarn at the seam.

Round 1 Work 4sc in row ends of each segment, ss in first sc, turn. *(64 sts.)*

Round 2 Work 1sc in each sc to end, ss in first sc. Fasten off.

TO FINISH

At the top of the beret, sew 16 beads on the first round, 8 beads on the 2nd round and four beads on the 3rd round. Weave in ends (see page 119).

TIPS

▨ To check your gauge, work the first segment. If it is the correct measurement, you can carry on. Try again with a smaller hook, if your segment was too large, or with a bigger hook, if your segment was too small.

▨ If you want a beret without beads, simply omit them and work a plain sc row between segments.

▨ Check that your beads have holes large enough to thread on to the yarn before buying them. If necessary, choose larger beads.

▨ The exact number of beads is given, but if you are buying glass beads by weight, you'll probably find that 3½oz (100g) will be enough. Plastic beads weigh less, so you may only need 1¾oz (50g).

▨ Try the beret on before working the brim edging. If you want a tighter fit, work fewer dc around the edge; if you want a looser fit, work more dc around edge.

▨ The beret here uses pearly pink beads to match the yarn, but you could choose beads in a contrasting color or select colors to match a favorite outfit.

Crochet Beads

These beads are simply round balls of firm single crochet, filled with batting, so they are very quick and easy to make—each bead case can take just minutes to crochet. Using coral and turquoise evokes the natural colors of semiprecious stones, while the smooth cotton embroidery yarn gives a lovely iridescent sheen. You can also enjoy experimenting with different yarns, such as metallics, for a fun, contemporary effect, and mixing and matching colors and textures.

ESTIMATED TIME TO COMPLETE

For the shell of one bead 10 minutes, without fiberfill and threading. For the necklace 2 hours; for the earrings about ½ hour.

YARN AND MATERIALS

Smooth mercerized perlé embroidery floss (100% cotton), 11yd (10m) per ¼oz (5g) hank. See tips for alternative yarn suggestions.
   1 hank in each of coral and turquoise

Polyester fiberfill or batting

Assorted white metal beads; 30 small round spacers; 14 medium beads and 7 large beads for the necklace; 4 small beads for the earrings

Barrel catch; nylon cord

2 earring hooks; 2 small jump rings; jewelry pliers

HOOK AND EQUIPMENT

B/1 (2.00mm) crochet hook

Large sharp needle

FINISHED MEASUREMENTS

Each bead approximately ¾in (2cm) across; **necklace length (adjustable)** 21½in (55cm)

GAUGE

16 sts measure 2⅜in (6cm), 7 rows measure approx 1¼in (3cm) over single crochet using B/1 (2.00mm) hook. Change hook size if necessary to obtain this gauge.

ABBREVIATIONS

cont = continue; **dec** = decrease; **sc** = single crochet; **ss** = slip stitch; **st(s)** = stitch(es); **[ ]** = work instructions in brackets as directed.

TIPS

■ Wind the hank of embroidery yarn into a ball so it doesn't get tangled.

■ You can use any fine, firm yarn to make beads. Mercerized cotton fingering (4ply) or metallic threads would also work well.

■ Adapt this design to suit yourself. Make a necklace using crochet beads alternated with small spacers; use a different shade of yarn for each pair of beads; make striped beads by changing color for each round. Create oval beads by working more rounds straight before the decrease round.

■ If you make a longer necklace, omit the catch and just join the ends at the back.

■ If you don't have jewelry pliers, you can use tweezers to attach the jump rings to the hooks.

■ Split jump rings are best for the earrings, but if you use ordinary rings don't pull the ends apart because this spoils the shape; always twist the ends in opposite directions, so that they'll line up neatly when you twist them back.

BEAD

Wind yarn around finger to make a ring.

Round 1 1ch, 8sc in ring, pull end to close ring, ss in first sc. *(8 sts.)*

Round 2 1ch, [2sc in each sc] to end, ss in first sc. *(16 sts.)*

Round 3 1ch, [1sc in each sc] to end, ss in first sc.

Round 3 forms sc. Cont in sc, work 3 more rounds.

Dec round 1ch, [miss 1sc, 1sc in next sc] 8 times, ss in first sc.

Leaving an end long enough to darn in, fasten off. Pack bead firmly with fiberfill or batting. Thread the thread end through the last round of sts, draw up, and secure. Weave the ends into the bead (see page 119).

NECKLACE

Using coral, make four beads as given above, then make two larger beads by working one extra sc round before the dec round, and two smaller beads by working the dec round after the 3rd round.

TO FINISH

Lay the beads out with a metal bead in the center, spacer beads on each side, then the large crochet beads on either side. Alternate spacers, metal and crochet beads, ending with spacers and small metal beads at each side and at the back neck. Attach half of the barrel catch to the end of the cord. Using the sharp needle to push through the crochet beads, thread the beads on to the cord, attach the other half of the barrel catch and thread the ends of the cord back through the beads before trimming.

EARRINGS

Using turquoise and working into the back loop of each stitch to give a ridged effect, make two beads, leaving long thread ends.

TO FINISH

Close the top of each bead, thread the end down to the bottom, slip on a small bead, then bring the end back to the top. Thread on a second small bead, knot the thread through the jump ring, and secure the end in the bead. Attach the jump rings to earring hooks.

Chapter 2
Sweaters & Tops

Shaded Blocks Sweater

Although the design of this clever sweater is based on a traditional granny square, the square is actually subtly shaped to make a flattering rectangle by working half double crochets instead of double crochet at each side on alternate rounds. The yarn is thick enough to work up quickly, yet it's soft and supple, so the sweater isn't heavy. The yoke, side panels, sleeves, and lower edging are all worked out from the blocks, so there's very little sewing required.

ESTIMATED TIME TO COMPLETE
For first size sweater, 18 hours.

YARN
Debbie Bliss Cashmerino Aran (55% merino wool, 33% acrylic, 12% cashmere) worsted (Aran) weight yarn, approx. 98yd (90m) per 1¾oz (50g) ball
2(**3**:4) balls in Navy 4 (A)
8(**9**:10) balls in Royal 612 (B)
3(**4**:4) balls in Silver 202 (C)
2(**3**:3) balls in White 25 (D)

HOOK AND EQUIPMENT
G/6 (4.50mm) crochet hook
Yarn needle

FINISHED MEASUREMENTS
To fit: bust 34 to 36(**38 to 40**:42 to 44)in
[86 to 91(**96 to 102**:107 to 112)cm]
Actual measurements:
bust 44(**47¼**:50½)in [112(**120**:128)cm];
length 26⅜(**27⅛**:28)in [67(**69**:71)cm];
sleeve 18in [46cm]
Figures in parentheses refer to larger sizes.
One figure refers to all sizes.

GAUGE
Four rounds of block measure 3¾ x 4½in (9.5 x 11cm); 17 rounds measure 17 x 20in (42 x 50cm); 14 sts and 10 rows to 4in (10cm) over half double crochet, using G/6 (4.50mm) hook. Change hook size if necessary to obtain this size block and gauge.

ABBREVIATIONS
ch = chain; **cont** = continue; **dc** = double crochet; **dec** = decrease; **foll** = following; **hdc** = half double crochet; **2hdctog** = yarn around hook, insert hook in first st and pull loop through, yarn around hook, insert hook in next st and pull loop through, yarn around hook and pull through 5 loops on hook; **patt** = pattern; **rep** = repeat; **RS** = right side; **sc** = single crochet; **sp** = space; **ss** = slip stitch; **st(s)** = stitch(es); **WS** = wrong side; **[ ]** = work instructions in brackets as directed.

TIPS
- To fasten off when working the squares, enlarge the last loop and pass the ball of yarn through. Where a color is used again after the next round, don't cut the yarn; carry it up on the back of the work until needed.
- You can save time at the end by weaving in or working over the ends as you go.

BLOCK
Using A, wind yarn around finger to form a ring.
Round 1 (RS) 6ch, [3dc in ring, 3ch] 3 times, 2dc in ring, pull end to close ring, ss in 3rd ch. Fasten off.
Round 2 Join B in first sp, 5ch, 3dc in same sp as join, * 2ch, 3dc in next 3ch sp, 3ch, 3hdc in same 3ch sp, 2ch *, 3hdc in next 3ch sp, 3ch, 3dc in same 3ch sp, rep from * to *, 2hdc in first sp, ss in 2nd ch. Fasten off.
Round 3 Join C in first sp, 6ch, 3dc in same sp as join, 2ch, [3dc in next 2ch sp, 2ch, 3dc in next 3ch sp, 3ch, 3dc in same 3ch sp, 2ch] 3 times, 3dc in next 2ch sp, 2ch, 2dc in first sp, ss in 3rd ch. Fasten off.
Round 4 Join D in first sp, 5ch, 3dc in same sp as join, 2ch, * [3dc in next 2ch sp, 2ch] twice, 3dc in next 3ch sp, 3ch, 3hdc in same 3ch sp, 2ch, [3hdc in next 2ch sp, 2ch] twice *, 3hdc in next 3ch sp, 3ch, 3dc in same 3ch sp, 2ch, rep from * to *, 2hdc in first sp, ss in 2nd ch. Fasten off.
Cont as Rounds 3 and 4. Working one more group and space on each side each time, work 13 more rounds in color order: C, B, A, B, C, D, C, B, A, B, C, D, C.
Fasten off.

BACK

Make block.

Yoke With RS facing you, placing joins in block at lower left and join B in top right corner sp.

Row 1 (RS) 3ch, 3dc in same sp as join, [3dc in each sp] to last sp, 4dc in last sp. 18 groups of sts. Change to A.

Row 2 1sc in first dc, 1ch, [1hdc in each dc] to last st, 1hdc in 3rd ch. *(56 sts.)*

Row 3 1sc in first hdc, 1ch, [1hdc in each hdc] to last st, 1hdc in ch **.
Row 3 forms hdc. Cont in hdc, work 4 rows B, 1 row A. Fasten off.

FRONT

Work as given for back to **.

Shape neck Cont in B.

Next row (WS) 1sc in first hdc, 1ch, 1hdc in each of next 12 hdc, turn and complete right side on these 13 sts. Cont in hdc, work 3 more rows B and 1 row A. Fasten off. With WS facing you, miss center 30 sts, join B in next st.

Next row 1sc in same place as join, 1ch, 1hdc in each hdc to last st, 1hdc in ch. *(13 sts.)*
Complete in same way as right side.

RIGHT SIDE PANEL

Matching stitches, join shoulder seams. With RS facing you, join B in lower right back corner sp.

Row 1 (RS) 1sc in same place as join, 1ch, [1hdc in each of next 3 dc, 1hdc in next sp] 17 times, 16 hdc across row ends of yoke, 1hdc in corner sp of front, [1hdc in each of next 3 dc, 1hdc in next sp] 17 times. *(154 sts.)*
Cont in hdc, work 3(**5**:7) more rows in B, 2 rows A, 1 row B.

Join sides With RS together and matching sts, insert hook through one st from each side together each time and work 52(**50**:48)sc. Fasten off.

LEFT SIDE PANEL

With RS facing you, join B in lower left front corner sp. Work as given for right side panel.

SLEEVES

With WS facing, join B at underarm.
Row 1 1sc in next st, 1ch, 1hdc in each of next 49(**53**:57) sts.
Cont in hdc and B on 50(**54**:58) sts, work two rows.
Dec row (RS) 1sc in first hdc, [1hdc in each hdc] to last 2 sts, 2hdctog. *(48(**52**:56) sts.)*
Cont in hdc and A, dec in this way at each end of 7 foll 4th rows. *(34(**38**:42) sts.)*
First size Work 1 row.
2nd size Dec one st at end of next row.
3rd size Dec one st at each end of next row.
All sizes *(34(**37**:40) sts.)*
Border. Row 1 (RS) 1sc in first hdc, 2ch, 1dc in same hdc, [2ch, miss 2hdc, 3dc in next hdc] 10(**11**:12) times, 2ch, miss 2hdc, 2dc in last st. Fasten off.
With RS facing, join A in 2nd ch.
Row 2 (RS) 1sc in 2nd ch, 4ch, [3dc in next sp, 2ch] to end, 1dc in last dc. Fasten off.
With RS facing, join B in first sp.
Row 3 [1sc, 2ch, 1dc] in first sp, [2ch, 3dc in next sp] to last sp, 2ch, 2dc in last sp.
Rows 2 and 3 form the border patt. Joining yarn with RS facing each time, work 1 row in each of C, D, C, B, A, and B. Do not fasten off after last row, turn.

Edging row (WS) 1sc in first dc, 1ch, 1hdc in next dc, [1hdc in next sp, 1hdc in each of next 3dc] to last 2dc, 1hdc in last sp, 1hdc in each of last 2dc. Fasten off. Weave in ends (see page 119).

LOWER EDGING

With RS facing, join B in back right corner sp.
Round 1 1sc in same place as join, 1ch, 1hdc in each dc across back, 1hdc in corner sp, 16(**19**:22)hdc in row ends of right side panel, 1hdc in corner sp, 1hdc in each dc across front, 1hdc in corner sp, 16(**19**:22)hdc in row ends of left side panel, ss in ch, turn. *(138(**144**:150) sts.)*
Round 2 1sc in same place as ss, 1ch, [1hdc in each hdc] to end, ss in ch, turn.
Turning each time, work 2(**4**:6) more rounds hdc.
Border. Round 1 (RS) 1sc in same place as ss, 4ch, [miss 2hdc, 3dc in next hdc, 2ch] to last 2 sts, 2dc in same place as sc, ss in 2nd ch.
Round 2 Ss in first sp, 1sc in first sp, 4ch, [3dc in next sp, 2ch] to end, 2dc in first sp, ss in 2nd ch.
Round 3 Ss in first sp, 1sc in first sp, 2ch, [3dc in next sp] to end, 2dc in first sp, ss in 2nd ch, turn.
Edging round (WS) 1sc in first dc, 1ch, [1hdc in each dc] to end, ss in ch. Fasten off. Weave in ends.

COLLAR

With RS facing, join A in first st at right back neck.
Round 1 (RS) 1sc in same st as join, 1ch, 1hdc in each of next 29 hdc, change to B, 5hdc in row ends down left front neck, 1hdc in each of 30hdc across front neck, 5hdc in row ends up right front neck, ss in ch. *(70 sts.)*
Cont in hdc, work 10 more rounds in B. Fasten off. Weave in ends.

TO FINISH

Press according to ball band.
Join sleeve seams.

Silver Top

Pretty picots add interest to the simplest chain mesh fabric of this stunning yet easy-to-work top.

ESTIMATED TIME TO COMPLETE

For the 2nd size top, 12 hours.

YARN

DMC Lumina Metallic Thread (40% polyester, 60% viscose) fingering (4-ply) weight yarn, approx. 164yd (150m) per ¾oz (25g) ball
   5(**6**:7:**8**) balls in Silver L168

HOOK AND EQUIPMENT

No. 6 steel (1.75mm) crochet hook

Yarn needle

FINISHED MEASUREMENTS

To fit: bust 81(**86**:91:**97**)cm [32(**34**:36:**38**)in]

Actual measurements:

bust 33(**36**:39½:**42½**)in [84(**92**:100:**108**)cm];
length 20¾(**21½**:22¼:**23¼**)in [53(**55**:56:**59**)cm]

Figures in parentheses refer to larger sizes. One figure refers to all sizes.

GAUGE

5 mesh spaces and 10 rows to 4in (10cm) over picot mesh patt, when pressed, using No. 6 steel (1.75mm) hook. Change hook size if necessary to obtain this gauge.

ABBREVIATIONS

ch = chain; **cont** = continue; **sc** = single crochet; **dec** = decrease; **tr** = treble; **patt** = pattern; **RS** = right side; **sp(s)** = space(s); **ss** = slip stitch; **WS** = wrong side; **[ ]** = work instructions in brackets as directed.

BACK

Picot edging 3ch, 1sc in first ch, [4ch, 1sc in 3rd ch] 42(**46**:50:**54**) times. *(43(**47**:51:**55**) picots)*
Work into straight edge.
Row 1 (WS) 1ch, 1sc in first picot, [6ch, miss 1 picot, 1sc in next picot, 3ch, ss in sc] to last 2 picots, 6ch, 1sc in last picot. *(21(**23**:25:**27**) mesh sps)*
Row 2 7ch, 1sc in first 6ch sp, 3ch, ss in sc, [6ch, 1sc in next 6ch sp, 3ch, ss in sc] to end, 3ch, 1tr in sc of previous row.
Row 3 1ch, 1sc in tr, [6ch, 1sc in next 6ch sp, 3ch, ss in sc] to last 6ch sp, 6ch, 1sc in 4th ch.
Row 4 7ch, 1sc in first 6ch sp, 3ch, ss in sc, [6ch, 1sc in next 6ch sp, 3ch, ss in sc] to end, 3ch, 1tr in sc.
Rows 3 and 4 form the picot mesh patt.

Cont in patt, work 30 more rows, ending with a 4th patt row.
Shape armholes. Row 1 1ch, 1sc in tr, 4ch, 1sc in first 6ch sp, [6ch, 1sc in next 6ch sp, 3ch, ss in sc] 18(**20**:22:**24**) times, 6ch, 1sc in next 6ch sp, 1tr in 4th ch, turn.
Dec row Ss in each of first 3ch, 1ch, 1sc in first sp, [6ch, 1sc in next 6ch sp, 3ch, ss in sc] 17(**19**:21:**23**) times, 6ch, 1sc in last 6ch sp.
Noting that instructions in brackets will be worked one less time on each row, work dec row 3 more times. 15(**17**:19:**21**) sps **.
Work 1 more dec row. *(14(**16**:18: **20**) sps)*
Patt 13(**15**:17:**19**) rows.
Finishing row 1ch, 1sc in tr, [4ch, 1sc in next sp] to last sp, 4ch, 1sc in 4th ch. Fasten off.

FRONT

Work as given for back to **.
Shape neck. Row 1 Ss in each of first 3ch, 1ch, 1sc in first sp, * [6ch, 1sc in next 6ch sp, 3ch, ss in sc] 6(**7**:8:**9**) times, 6ch *, 1sc in center sp, rep from * to *, 6ch, 1sc in last sp.
Row 2 7ch, 1sc in first 6ch sp, [3ch, ss in sc, 6ch, 1sc in next 6ch sp] 5(**6**:7:**8**) times, 3ch, ss in sc, 3ch, 1tr in 3rd ch, turn and complete right side.
Row 3 6ch, 1sc in next 6ch sp, [3ch, ss in sc, 6ch, 1sc in next 6ch sp] 4(**5**:6:**7**) times, 3ch, ss in sc, 6ch, 1sc in 3rd ch. *(6(**7**:8:**9**) sps)*
Noting that instructions in brackets will be worked one time fewer on each row, work Rows 2 and 3 three more times. *(3(**4**:5:**6**) sps)*

Next row 7ch, 1sc in first sp, [3ch, ss in sc, 6ch, 1sc in next sp] 2(**3**:4:**5**) times, 3ch, ss in sc, 3ch, 1tr in 3rd ch.

Cont in patt, work 4(**6**:8:**10**) rows straight.

Work finishing row in same way as back.

With WS facing, join yarn in 6ch sp at left of center for left side.

Row 1 6ch, [1sc in next 6ch sp, 3ch, ss in sc, 6ch] 5(**6**:7:**8**) times, 3ch, ss in sc, 3ch, 1tr in tr.

Row 2 1ch, 1sc in tr, [6ch, 1sc in next 6ch sp, 3ch, ss in sc] 5(**6**:7:**8**) times, 3ch, 1tr in 3rd ch.

Noting that instructions in brackets will be worked one less time on each row, work Rows 1 and 2 three more times. *(3(**4**:5:**6**) sps)*

Patt 5(**7**:9:**11**) rows straight.

Work finishing row in same way as back.

EDGING

Matching sts, join shoulders. Join yarn at right shoulder and work a round of sc and picots evenly around neck edge. Finish armholes in the same way.

TO FINISH

Press according to ball band. Join side seams.

TIPS

■ This yarn is quite slippery, so keep a rubber band on the ball, releasing just enough yarn to work a single row at a time.

■ For extra control, wind the yarn one or two times around the middle finger of the left hand to add tension.

■ The fabric looks the same on both sides, but the edge stitches are different, so mark the right side of the work to make it easier to count the rows as you shape the armholes and neck.

Cardigan with Lacy Edging

This gently fitted cardigan flatters the figure with its sophisticated style, while its simple stitch pattern combines single and double crochet. The openwork bands go quickly, along with the rows of single crochet, which create tighter spacing. The pretty lacy edging looks complex but is actually worked in just three rows.

ESTIMATED TIME TO COMPLETE

For the first size cardigan, 25 hours.

YARN

Debbie Bliss Rialto 4 Ply (100% merino wool) fingering (4-ply) weight yarn, approx. 197yd (180m) per 1¾oz (50g) ball
  7(**8**:9:**10**) balls in Red 9

HOOK AND EQUIPMENT

D/3 (3.00mm) and C/2 (2.50mm) crochet hooks
Yarn needle

FINISHED MEASUREMENTS

To fit: bust 32–34(**36–38**:40–42:**44–46**)in [81–86(**91–97**:102–107:**112–117**)cm]

Actual measurements: bust 35(**39½**:44: **48½**)in [89(**100.5**:112:**123.5**)cm]; **length** 21½(**22**:23½:**24**)in [55(**56**:60:**61**)cm]; **sleeve** 18½in [47cm]

Figures in parentheses refer to larger sizes. One figure refers to all sizes.

GAUGE

21 sts and 16 rows to 4in (10cm) over patt, when pressed, using D/3 (3.00mm) hook. Change hook size if necessary to obtain this gauge.

ABBREVIATIONS

beg = beginning; **ch** = chain; **cont** = continue; **dc** = double crochet; **2dctog** = leaving last loop of each stitch on the hook, work 2dc, yoh and pull through 3 loops on hook; **3dctog** = leaving last loop of each stitch on the hook, work 3dc, yoh and pull through 4 loops on hook; **dec** = decrease; **3trcl** = leaving last loop of each stitch on the hook, work 3 treble sts, yoh and pull through 4 loops on hook; **foll** = following; **inc** = increase; **patt** = pattern; **RS** = right side; **sc** = single crochet; **sp(s)** = space(s); **ss** = slip stitch; **st(s)** = stitch(es); **WS** = wrong side; **yoh** = yarn over hook; **[ ]** = work instructions in brackets as directed.

NOTE

The fronts are two rows longer than the back, so that the pattern will match at the shoulders.

TIPS

- Use a larger hook to work the starting chain loosely and evenly, changing to a D/3 (3.00mm) hook for the last 3ch to keep them neat.

- It's easy to see which side of the work you're on, because all wrong-side rows are in single crochet, while all right-side rows use double crochet stitches.

- You'll find it easy to keep track of the side and sleeve shaping if you mark each end of the decrease and increase rows.

BACK

Using D/3 (3.00mm) hook, make 89(**101**:113:**125**)ch.
Row 1 (RS) 1dc in 4th ch from hook, [1dc in each ch] to end. (87(**99**:111:**123**) sts.)
Row 2 1ch, [1sc in each dc] to last st, 1sc in top ch.
Row 3 1sc in first sc, 3ch, [miss 1sc, 1dc in next sc, 1ch] to end.

Row 4 1sc in first dc, [1sc in 1ch sp, 1sc in next dc] to end, working last sc in 2nd ch.
Row 5 1sc in first sc, 2ch, [1dc in each sc] to end.
Rows 2 to 5 form the patt.
Patt 3 more rows.
Dec row (RS) 1sc in first sc, 2ch, 3dctog, [1dc in each sc] to last 4 sc, 3dctog, 1dc in last sc. (83(**95**:107:**119**) sts.)

Patt 3 rows, then work dec row again. (79(**91**:103:**115**) sts.)
Patt 15 rows.

Inc row (RS) 1sc in first sc, 2ch, 3dc in next sc, 1dc in each sc to last 2 sc, 3dc in next sc, 1dc in last sc. (83(**95**:107:**119**) sts.)
Cont in patt, inc in this way at each end of 2 foll 8th rows. (91(**103**:115:**127**) sts.)
Patt 9(**9**:13:**13**) rows.

Shape armholes.

Row 1 (RS) Ss in each of first 4(**4**:6:**6**) dc, [1sc, 3ch] in next sc, [miss 1sc, 1dc in next sc, 1ch] to last 4(**4**:6:**6**) sc, turn.

Row 2 1sc in first dc, [1sc in 1ch sp, 1sc in next st] to end. *(83(**95**:103:**115**) sts.)*

Row 3 1sc in first sc, 2ch, 3dctog, 1dc in each sc to last 4 sc, 3dctog, 1dc in last sc.

Row 4 1ch, [1sc in each st] to end.

Row 5 [1sc, 2ch] in first sc, [miss 1sc, 1dc in next sc, 1ch] to last 4 sc, miss 1sc, placing first part dc in next sc and 2nd part dc in last sc, work 2dctog.

Row 6 1ch, 1sc in 2dctog, [1sc in next ch sp, 1sc in foll dc] to end.

Cont in patt, dec in same way as Rows 3 and 5 on next 1(**2**:3:**4**) RS rows. *(71(**79**:83:**91**) sts.)*

Patt 25 rows. Fasten off.

LEFT FRONT

Using D/3 (3.00mm) hook, make 43(**49**:55:**61**)ch.

Work Row 1 as given for back. *(41(**47**:53:**59**) sts.)*

Work in patt as given for back for 7 more rows.

Dec row (RS) 1sc in first sc, 2ch, 3dctog, [1dc in each sc] to end. *(39(**45**:51:**57**) sts.)*

Patt 3 rows then work dec row again. *(37(**43**:49:**55**) sts.)*

Patt 15 rows.

Inc row (RS) 1sc in first sc, 2ch, 3dc in next sc, [1dc in each sc] to end. *(39(**45**:51:**57**) sts.*

Cont in patt, inc in this way at beg of 2 foll 8th rows. *(43(**49**:55:**61**) sts.)*

Patt 9(**9**:13:**13**) rows.

Shape armhole and neck.

Row 1 (RS) Ss in each of first 4(**4**:6:**6**) sc, [1sc, 3ch] in next sc, miss 1sc, 1dc in next sc, [1ch, miss 1sc, 1dc in next sc] to end. *(39(**45**:49:**55**) sts.*

Rows 2 to 6 Work as given for Rows 2 to 6 of back armhole shaping. *(31(**37**:41:**47**) sts.)*

Cont in patt, dec as set at each end of next 1(**2**:2:**2**) RS rows. *(27(**29**:33:**39**) sts.)*

1st and 2nd sizes Cont in patt, dec in same way as before at end of 5 foll 4th rows.

3rd size Dec at beg of next RS row, at neck edge on foll RS row, then at neck edge on 4 foll 4th rows.

4th size Dec at beg of next RS row, at each end of foll RS row and at neck edge on 5 foll 4th rows.

All sizes 17(**19**:21:**23**) sts.)

Patt 7(**7**:9:**7**) rows. Fasten off. Weave in ends (see page 119).

RIGHT FRONT

Using D/3 (3.00mm) hook, make 43(**49**:55:**61**)ch.

Work Row 1 as given for back. *(41(**47**:53:**59**) sts.)*

Work in patt as given for back for 7 more rows.

Dec row (RS) 1sc in first sc, 2ch, [1dc in each sc] to last 4 sc, 3dctog, 1dc in last sc. *(39(**45**:51:**57**) sts.)*

Patt 3 rows, then work dec row again.
*(37(**43**:49:**55**) sts.)*
Patt 15 rows.

Inc row (RS) 1sc in first sc, 2ch,
1dc in each sc to last 2 sc, 3dc in next
sc, 1dc in last sc. *39(**45**:51:**57**) sts.)*
Cont in patt, inc in this way at end
of 2 foll 8th rows. *(43(**49**:51:**61**) sts.)*
Patt 9(**9**:13:**13**) rows.

Shape armhole and neck.

Row 1 (RS) 1sc in first sc, 3ch, miss
1sc, 1dc in next sc, [1ch, miss 1sc,
1dc in next sc] to last 4(4:6:6) sc, turn.
*(39(**45**:49:**55**) sts.)*

Rows 2 to 6 Work as given for Rows
2 to 6 of back armhole shaping.
31(**37**:41:**47**) sts.
Cont in patt, dec as set at each end
of next 1(**2**:2:**2**) RS rows.
*(27(**29**:33:**39**) sts.)*

1st and 2nd sizes Cont in patt, dec
in same way as before at beg of 5 foll
4th rows.

3rd size Dec at end of next RS row,
at neck edge on foll RS row, then at
neck edge on 4 foll 4th rows.

4th size Dec at end of next RS row,
at each end of foll RS row and at
neck edge on 5 foll 4th rows.

All sizes 17(**19**:21:**23**) sts.
Patt 7(**7**:9:**7**) rows. Fasten off. Weave
in ends.

SLEEVES

Using D/3 (3.00mm) hook, make
(43(**47**:51:**55**)ch.
Work Row 1 as given for back.
*(41(**45**:49:**53**) sts.)*
Work 11 more rows in patt as given
for back.
Cont in patt, inc in same way as
back at each end of next row and
on 6(**6**:7:**7**) foll 8th rows.
*(69(**73**:81:**85**) sts.)*
Patt 13(**13**:5:**5**) rows.

Shape top Work as given for Rows 1
to 6 of back armhole shaping.
Cont in patt, dec in same way as Rows
3 and 5 of back on next 1(**2**:3:**4**)
RS rows. *(49 sts.)*
Cont in patt, dec as before at each
end of 3 foll 4th rows, then at each end
of next 3 RS rows. *(25 sts.)*
Work 1 row. Fasten off.

LACY EDGING

Matching sts, join shoulders.
Using C/2 (2.50mm) hook and with
RS facing, join yarn at lower edge of
right front.

Row 1 (RS) Work 132(**136**:142:**146**)
sc up right front edge, 34(**35**:41:**42**)
sc across back neck and
132(**136**:142:**146**)sc down left front
edge. *(298(**307**:325:**334**) sts.)*

Row 2 1ch, 1sc in first sc, 4ch, miss
2sc, [1dc in next sc, 2ch, miss 2sc]
to last sc, 1dc in last sc.

Row 3 [6ch, 1dc in first ch, miss
first sp, 3trcl in next sp, 6ch, 1dc in
first ch, 3trcl in same sp, 6ch, 1dc in
next ch, miss next sp, 1sc in next dc]
33(**34**:36:**37**) times.
Fasten off. Weave in ends (see
page 119).

CUFF EDGINGS

Using C/2 (2.50mm) hook and with
WS facing, join yarn and work 1sc in
each starting ch. *(41(**45**:49:**53**) sts.)*
Picot row (RS) 1sc in first sc, [6ch, ss
in first ch, 1sc in each of next 2sc] to
end. Fasten off. Weave in ends.

TO FINISH

Press lightly. Join side and sleeve
seams. Set in sleeves. Finish lower
edge of cardigan in same way as
cuffs. Make a 24in (61cm) length
of chain. Fasten off. Slip through
lace edging and tie.

Silk Sampler Jacket

The bands of lacy pattern may look complex, but they're made with just the basic crochet stitches. Because the jacket is made in one piece to the armholes, the patterns match all the way around. By the time you shape the neck, you're familiar with the patterns, so you'll have an instinctive feel for where the patterns break, and the sleeves are the simplest mesh.

ESTIMATED TIME TO COMPLETE

For the first size, 20 hours.

YARN

Sirdar Snuggly Cashmere Merino Silk DK (75% merino wool, 20% silk, 5% cashmere) light worsted (DK) weight yarn, approx. 127yd (116m) per 1¾oz (50g) ball
9(11:13) balls in Pied Piper 305

HOOK AND EQUIPMENT

G/6 (4.50mm) crochet hook

Yarn needle

FINISHED MEASUREMENTS

To fit: bust 32 to 34(**36 to 38**:40 to 42)in [81 to 86(**91 to 97**:102 to 107)cm]

Actual measurements: bust 37(**41½**:46) in [94(**105.5**:117)cm]; length 26(**26¾**:28)in [66(**68**:71)cm]; **sleeve** 18in (46cm)

Figures in parentheses refer to larger sizes. One figure refers to all sizes.

GAUGE

21 sts to 4in (10cm) over single crochet, 6 rows of shell patt measure 3½in (9cm), 6 rows of mesh patt measure 2¾in (7cm), 8 rows of fan patt measure 2¾in (7cm), all when pressed using G/6 (4.50mm) hook. Change hook size if necessary to obtain these gauges.

ABBREVIATIONS

beg = beginning; **ch** = chain; **cont** = continue; **dc** = double crochet; **2dctog** = leaving last loop of each st on hook, work 2dc, yoh and pull through 3 loops on hook; **patt** = pattern; **rep** = repeat; **sc** = single crochet; **2sctog** = insert hook in first st and pull loop through, insert hook in next st and pull loop through, yoh and pull through 3 loops on hook; **sp** = space; **ss** = slip stitch; **st(s)** = stitch(es); **tr** = treble; **yoh** = yarn over hook; **[ ]** = work instructions in brackets as directed.

NOTE

The jacket is worked in one piece to the armholes, then divided for the fronts and the back.

TIPS

- The chain stitches, especially when working the mesh pattern, should be neat but not too tight. If you work tightly, you may need to add an extra chain to create a flexible fabric.

- If you'd like to make a matching covered button from leftover yarn, you'll need a smooth domed button or a button mould and a C/2 (2.50mm) crochet hook. Wind yarn around finger to form a ring, work 8sc in ring, then continue in a spiral working 2sc in each sc until cover is almost the same size as the button, work a few rounds without increasing, then miss alternate sc until cover fits over button. Insert button and work 2sctog in remaining sc until gap is as small as possible. Fasten off, thread end of yarn through stitches, draw up, and secure.

BACK AND FRONTS

Scallop edging. Row 1 [Make 10ch, ss in first ch to form a ring, 9sc in ring] 32(**36**:40) times, turn.

Row 2 1ch, [1sc in each sc] to end, do not turn. Work in patt along top edge.

Row 1 (RS) 1ch, 1sc in row end of first sc, [5sc in sp, 1sc between scallops] 31(**35**:39) times, 5sc in last sp, 1sc in row end of last sc. *(193(**217**:241) sts.)*

Row 2 1ch, [1sc in each sc] to end. This row forms sc. Work 1 more row sc.

Row 4 1ch, 1sc in first sc, 2ch, * miss 2sc, [3dc, 1ch, 3dc] in next sc, miss 2sc, 1dc in next sc, rep from * 31(**35**:39) more times.

Row 5 1sc in first dc, 4ch, [1sc in 1ch sp, 2ch, miss 3dc, 1dc in next dc, 2ch] to end, omitting last 2ch and working last dc in 2nd ch.

Row 6 1sc in first dc, 2ch, 3dc in same dc as sc, [1dc in next sc, 3dc in next dc, 1ch, 3dc in same dc] to last dc, 1dc in last sc, 4dc in 2nd ch.

Row 7 1sc in first dc, [2ch, miss 3dc, 1dc in next dc, 2ch, 1sc in 1ch sp] to end, working last sc in 2nd ch.

Row 8 1sc in first sc, 2ch, * [3dc, 1ch, 3dc] in next dc, 1dc in next sc, rep from * to end.

Row 9 As Row 5.

Rows 4 to 9 form shell patt.

Row 10 1ch, 1sc in first dc, [2sc in 2ch sp, 1sc in sc, 2sc in 2ch sp, 1sc in dc] to end, working last sc in 2nd ch. *(193(**217**:241) sts.)*
Work 1 row sc.

Row 12 1ch, 1sc in first sc, [6ch, miss 2sc, 1sc in next sc] to end.

Row 13 5ch, 1sc in first 6ch sp, [2ch, 1sc in next 6ch sp] to last sp, 2ch, 1dc in sc.

Row 14 1ch, 1sc in dc, 6ch, miss first 2ch sp, [1sc in next 2ch sp, 6ch] to end, 1sc in 3rd ch.

Rows 15, 16, and 17 As Rows 13, 14, and 13.
Rows 12 to 17 form mesh patt.

Row 18 1ch, 1sc in dc, 1sc in first 2ch sp, [1sc in next sc, 2sc in next 2ch sp] to last 2ch sp, 1sc in last sc, 1sc in 5ch sp, 1sc in 3rd ch. *(193(**217**:241) sts.)*

Row 19 1ch, [1sc in each sc] to end.

Row 20 1ch, 1sc in first sc, * 2ch, miss 2sc, 1sc in next sc, 1ch, miss 2sc, [2dctog, 1ch] 3 times in next sc, miss 2sc, 1sc in next sc, 2ch, miss 2sc, 1sc in next sc, rep from * to end.

Row 21 1ch, 1sc in first sc, 1ch, * 1sc in next 2ch sp, 1ch, [2dctog in next 1ch sp, 1ch] 4 times, 1sc in next 2ch sp, 1ch, rep from * to end, omitting last ch.

Row 22 1ch, 1sc in first sc, 8ch, [1sc in 1ch sp between center pair of 2dctog, 5ch, 1tr in 1ch sp between 2sc, 5ch] to end, omitting last 5ch and working last tr in last sc.

Row 23 1ch, 1sc in tr, [5sc in next 5ch sp, 1sc in sc, 5sc in foll 5ch sp, 1sc in tr] to end. *(193(**217**:241) sts.)*

Rows 24, 25, 26, 27, 28, and 29
As Rows 19, 20, 21, 22, 23, and 19.
*(193(**217**:241) sts.)*
Rows 20 to 27 form fan patt.
Work Rows 12 to 19, then Rows 4 to 11 again.

Left front. Row 1 (WS) 1ch, 1sc in first sc, [6ch, miss 2sc, 1sc in next sc] 14(**16**:18) times, turn.

Row 2 5ch, 1sc in first ch sp, [2ch, 1sc in next ch sp] 13(**15**:17) times.

Row 3 1ch, 1sc in first sp, [6ch, 1sc in next sp] 12(**14**:16) times, 6ch, 1sc in 3rd ch.

Row 4 5ch, 1sc in first sp, [2ch, 1sc in next sp] 12(**14**:16) times.

Row 5 1ch, 1sc in first sp, [6ch, 1sc in next sp] 11(**13**:15) times, 6ch, 1sc in 3rd ch.

Row 6 5ch, 1sc in first sp, [2ch, 1sc in next sp] 11(**13**:15) times.

Row 7 1ch, 2sc in first sp, [1sc in next sc, 2sc in next sp] 10(**12**:14) times, 1sc in next sc, 1sc in last sp, 1sc in 3rd ch.

Row 8 1ch, 1sc in each sc to last 2sc, 2sctog. *(34(**40**:46) sts.)*

Row 9 1ch, [miss 1sc, 1sc in next sc] twice, * 2ch, miss 2sc, 1sc in next sc, 1ch, miss 2sc, [2dctog, 1ch] 3 times in next sc, miss 2sc, 1sc in next sc, 2ch, miss 2sc, 1sc in next sc, rep from * 1(**2**:2) times, 1st and 3rd sizes 2ch, miss 2sc, 1sc in next sc, 1ch, miss 2sc, [2dctog, 1ch, 2dctog] in last sc.

Row 10. 1st and 3rd sizes 1sc in first 2dctog, 3ch, [2dctog in next 1ch sp, 1ch] twice, all sizes patt as Row 21 until sc in last 2ch sp has been completed, 1ch, 1sc in sc, ss in last sc.

Row 11 1ch, 1sc in first 1ch sp, 6ch, 1sc in 1ch sp between center pair of 2dctog, patt as Row 22, 1st and 3rd sizes ending 1sc in 2nd ch.

Row 12. 1st and 3rd sizes 1ch, 1sc in first sc, all sizes work Row 23 to last sc in 1ch sp, 3sc in 6ch sp. *(28(**34**:40) sts.)*

Row 13 1ch, miss first sc, [1sc in each sc] to end. *(27(**33**:39) sts.)*

Row 14. 1st and 3rd sizes 3ch, [2dctog, 1ch] twice in first sc, all sizes patt as Row 20 until 2nd 2dctog of last motif has been completed, 1tr in last sc.

Row 15 1ch, 1sc in first 2dctog, 4ch, [2dctog in next 1ch sp, 1ch] twice, patt as Row 21, 1st and 3rd sizes ending 1dc in last 2dctog.

Row 16. 1st and 3rd sizes 1ch, 1sc in first 1ch sp, all sizes patt as Row 22 until last tr in 1ch sp is complete. 4ch, sc in 4ch sp.

Row 17 1ch, miss first sc, 4sc in 4ch sp, patt as Row 23 to end.

Row 18 1ch, [1sc in each sc] to last 2sc, 2sctog. *(22(**28**:34) sts.)*

Beg with Row 12, cont in patt, work 6(**8**:10) rows, then work Rows 17, 18, and 19. Fasten off.

Back With WS facing, leave 11sc for left armhole, join yarn in next st.

Row 1 1ch, 1sc in same place as join, [6ch, miss 2sc, 1sc in next sc] 28(**32**:36) times, turn.

Cont in patt until back matches front to shoulder, 1st and 3rd sizes Working half repeats at ends of rows where necessary in same way as given for left front. Fasten off.

Right front With WS facing, leave 11sc of right armhole, join yarn in next st.

Row 1 1ch, 1sc in same place as join, [6ch, miss 2sc, 1sc in next sc] 13(**15**:17) times, 3ch, miss 2sc, 1dc in last sc.

Row 2 1sc in first sp, [2ch, 1sc in next sp] to end, 1ch, 1dc in last sc. Beg and ending in this way, patt 4 more rows.

Row 7 1sc in dc, miss 1ch sp, [1sc in next sc, 2sc in next 2ch sp] to end, 1sc in last sc. *(35(**41**:47) sts.)*

Row 8 1ch, miss first sc, [1sc in each sc] to end. *(34(**40**:46) sts.)*

Row 9. 1st and 3rd sizes 3ch, [2dctog, 1ch] twice in first sc, **all sizes** patt as Row 20 until last group of 2dctog, 1ch is complete, miss 2sc, 1sc in next sc, 2ch, miss 2sc, 1sc in next sc, 1ch, miss 1sc, 1sc in foll sc.

Row 10 1ch, 1sc in 1ch sp, 1ch, 1sc in next sp, patt as Row 21, 1st and 3rd sizes ending 1dc in last 2dctog.

Row 11. 1st and 3rd sizes 1ch, 1sc in dc, all sizes patt as Row 22 until last sc in center sp of last group of 2dctog, has been completed, 3ch, 1tr in last sc.

Row 12 1ch, miss tr, 3sc in 3ch sp, patt as Row 23, 1st and 3rd sizes ending 1sc in last sc. *(28(**34**:40) sts.)*

Row 13 1ch, [1sc in each sc] to last 2sc, 2sctog. *(27(**33**:39) sts.)*

Row 14 Ss in first sc, 4ch, miss 2sc, [2dctog, 1ch] twice in next sc, patt as Row 20, 1st and 3rd sizes ending [1ch, 2dctog] twice in last sc, 1dc in last sc.

Row 15. 1st and 3rd sizes 1sc in first 2dctog, 3ch, **all sizes** patt as Row 21 until 2nd 2dctog, 1ch of last motif have been completed, 1tr in 4th ch.

Row 16 1sc in tr, 4ch, patt as Row 22, 1st and 3rd sizes ending 1sc in 3ch sp.

Row 17 Patt as Row 23 until sc in last tr is complete, 3sc in last 4ch sp, 1sc in last sc.

Row 18 1ch, [1sc in each sc] to last 2sc, 2sctog. *(22(**28**:34) sts.)*

Complete to match left front.

SLEEVES

Matching sts, join shoulders. With RS facing, work 94(**103**:112) sc evenly along row ends of armhole edge. Repeating Rows 12 and 13 to form mesh patt, work in mesh patt for 6 rows.

Shape sleeve. Row 1 1sc in first sc, [6ch, 1sc in next 2ch sp] to last 2ch sp, 3ch, 1dc in 3rd ch.

Row 2 1ch, 1sc in first sp, [2ch, 1sc in next 6ch sp] to last 6ch sp.

Row 3 1ch, 1sc in first sp, [6ch, 1sc in next 2ch sp] until one 2ch sp remains, [yoh] twice, insert hook in last 2ch sp, then in last sc, [yoh, pull through] 3 times.

Work last 2 rows 5(**6**:7) more times.

Next row 1ch, 1sc in first sp, [6ch, 1sc in next sp] to end, 1sc in last sc. Cont in patt, work 22(**20**:18) more rows.

2nd size Decreasing 3 sts evenly across row, all sizes work 1 row sc in same way as Row 15 of back and fronts. *(52(**52**:58) sts.)*

Edging. Row 1 1sc in each of first 3sc, [5ch, miss 3sc, 1sc in each of next 3sc] to end, 1sc in last sc.

Row 2 1ch, miss first sc, ss in next sc, miss 1sc, [9sc in 5ch sp, miss 1sc, ss in next sc, miss 1sc] to end, ss in last sc.

Row 3 Miss first sc, [1sc in each of next 9 sc, 1sc in sc with ss of 2nd row] to end, ending ss in last sc. Fasten off. Weave in ends (see page 119).

FRONT EDGING

With RS facing, work 262(**274**:286)sc evenly up right front edge, around neck and down left front edge. Work edging as given for sleeves.

TO FINISH

Press according to ball band. Join row ends at top of sleeves to 11 sts left at underarms and join sleeve seams. Join ends of edgings. Weave in ends.

Aran-Style Coat

The stitch pattern of this slightly flared three-quarter-length coat couldn't be simpler—it's just alternate rows of double and single crochet. Double crochet rows make it grow quickly, while the single crochet adds stability to the fabric. The Aran-effect pattern of raised lines and bobbles is made by working surface-chain diamonds and bobbles, so you can add more decoration to your coat or just leave it plain.

ESTIMATED TIME TO COMPLETE

For the 2nd size coat, 28 hours.

YARN AND MATERIALS

Debbie Bliss Cashmerino Aran (55% merino wool, 33% acrylic, 12% cashmere) worsted (Aran) weight yarn, approx. 98yd (90m) per 1¾oz (50g) ball

  20(21:22:23:24:25:26:27) balls in Ecru 101

5 buttons

HOOK AND EQUIPMENT

H/8 (5.00mm) and J/10 (6.00mm) crochet hooks

Yarn needle

FINISHED MEASUREMENTS

To fit: bust 32(34:36:38:40:42:44:46)in [81(86:91:97:102:107:112:117)cm]

Actual measurements: bust 34(36¼:38½: 40¾:43:45¼:47½:49¾)in [86.5(92.5:98: 103.5:109.5:115:121:126.5)cm];
length 30½(31½:31½:32¼:33¼:34:34:35)in [77.5(80:80:82:84.5:86.5:86.5:89)cm];
sleeve 19¼in [49cm]

Figures in parentheses refer to larger sizes. One figure refers to all sizes.

GAUGE

14 sts and 9 rows to 4in (10cm) over double and single crochet pattern, when pressed, using J/10 (6.00mm) hook. Change hook size if necessary to obtain this gauge.

ABBREVIATIONS

beg = beginning; **ch** = chain; **cont** = continue; **dc** = double crochet; **2dctog** = leaving last loop of each st on hook, work 2dc, yoh and pull through 3 loops on hook; **dec** = decrease; **foll** = following; **inc** = increase; **patt** = pattern; **RS** = right side; **sp** = space; **sc** = single crochet; **2sctog** = insert hook in next st, yoh and pull through, insert hook in foll st, yoh and pull through, yoh and pull through 3 loops on hook; **ss** = slip stitch; **st(s)** = stitch(es); **WS** = wrong side; **yoh** = yarn over hook; **[ ]** = work instructions in brackets as directed.

BACK

Welt. Ribbing Using H/8 (5.00mm) hook, make 13ch.

Row 1 (RS) 1dc in 4th ch from hook, [1dc in each ch] to end. *(11 sts.)*

Row 2 1ch, miss first dc, [1sc around stem of each st] to end. *(10 sts.)*

Row 3 3ch, [1dc in each sc] to end. *(11 sts.)*

Rows 2 and 3 form the ribbing patt. Work 68(72:76:80:84:88:92:96) more rows, ending with a Row 3.

Do not fasten off; turn and work along row ends.

Edging. Row 1 (RS) 1ch, 2sc in first dc, [1sc in next ridge, 1sc in next dc] to end, 1sc in end ch.

Row 2 1ch, [1sc around stem of each sc] to end, 1sc around end ch. *(74(78:82:86:90:94:98:102) sts.)*

Change to J/10 (6.00mm) hook.

Row 1 (RS) 1sc in first sc, 2ch, [1dc in each sc] to end.

Row 2 1ch, [1sc in each dc] to end, 1sc in 2nd ch.

These 2 rows form the dc and sc patt.

Dec row (RS) 1sc in first sc, 2ch, 1dc in next sc, 2dctog, [1dc in each sc] to last 4sc, 2dctog, 1dc in each of last 2sc.

Cont in dc and sc patt, dec in this way at each end of 7 foll 4th rows. *(58(62:66:70:74:78:82:86) sts.)*

Patt 13(13:13:13:15:15:15:15) rows.

Shape armholes. Next row (RS)
Ss in each of first 2(**3**:3:**4**:4:**5**:5:**6**)
sc, 1sc in next sc, 2ch, [1dc in each
sc] to last 2(**3**:3:**4**:4:**5**:5:**6**)sc, turn.
*(54(**56**:60:**62**:66:**68**:72:**74**) sts.)*
Cont in dc and sc patt, dec in
same way as before at each end
of next 2(**2**:3:**3**:4:**4**:5:**5**) **RS rows.**
*(50(**52**:54:**56**:58:**60**:62:**64**) sts.)*
Patt 13(**15**:13:**15**:13:**15**:13:**15**) rows.
Fasten off. Weave in ends (see
page 119).

LEFT FRONT
Ribbing Work as given for back
ribbing until 35(**37**:39:**41**:43:**45**:47:**49**)
rows have been completed.
Work 1st and 2nd edging
rows as given for back.
*(38(**40**:42:**44**:46:**48**:50:**52**) sts.)*
Change to J/10 (6.00mm) hook.
Work 2 rows in dc and sc patt as given
for back **.
Dec row (RS) 1sc in first sc, 2ch,
1dc in next sc, 2dctog, [1dc in each
sc] to end.
Cont in dc and sc patt, dec in
this way at beg of 7 foll 4th rows.
*(30(**32**:34:**36**:38:**40**:42:**44**) sts.)*
Patt 13(**13**:13:**13**:15:**15**:15:**15**) rows.
Shape armhole. Next row (RS)
Ss in each of first 2(**3**:3:**4**:4:**5**:5:**6**)sc,
1sc in next sc, 2ch, [1dc in each sc]
to end. *(28(**29**:31:**32**:34:**35**:37:**38**)
sts.)*
Cont in dc and sc patt, dec in
same way as before at beg of
next 2(**2**:3:**3**:4:**4**:5:**5**) RS rows.
*(26(**27**:28:**29**:30:**31**:32:**33**) sts.)*
Patt 5(**7**:5:**7**:5:**7**:5:**7**) rows.
Shape neck. Row 1 (RS) 1sc in
first sc, 2ch, 1dc in each of next
12(**13**:14:**15**:15:**16**:17:**18**)sc, 2dctog,
1dc in each of next 2sc, turn and leave
9(**9**:9:**9**:10:**10**:10:**10**)sc free for neck.
*(16(**17**:18:**19**:19:**20**:21:**22**) sts.)*
Row 2 1ch, 2sctog, 1sc in each
st to end.

- The coat shown here has panels of decoration only on the front; the back of the jacket is plain. If you prefer a more detailed design, you could add more lines of bobbles to each of the front panels or work panels on the back and the sleeves, too. Remember that if you do, you may need some additional yarn.

- If, on the other hand, you decide not to work the decorative panels on your coat at all, you may be able to get away with one fewer ball of yarn.

- Working around the stem of a stitch tips the chain edge to the right side, giving a rib effect. Simply insert the hook from right to left, in and out again behind the stem at the top of the double crochet to work the sc stitch.

- When working the surface bobbles, you may find it easier to bring your left hand on top to work the 5ch.

- It's easy to see which side of the work you're on, because all RS rows are dc rows.

- All side and sleeve shapings are made on RS rows. Mark the shaping rows to help keep count of how many pairs of increases or decreases you've worked.

Row 3 1sc in first sc, 2ch, 1dc in each sc to last 4sc, 2dctog, 1dc in each of last 2sc.
Row 4 As Row 2.
(13(14:15:16:16:17:18:19) sts.)
Patt 4 rows. Fasten off. Weave in ends.

RIGHT FRONT

Work as given for left front to **.
Dec row (RS) 1sc in first sc, 2ch, [1dc in each sc] to last 4sc, 2dctog, 1dc in each of last 2sc.
Cont in dc and sc patt, dec in this way at end of 7 foll 4th rows.
(30(32:34:36:38:40:42:44) sts.)
Patt 13(13:13:13:15:15:15:15) rows.

Shape armhole. Next row (RS)
1sc in first sc, 2ch, [1dc in each sc] to last 2(3:3:4:4:5:5:6)sc, turn.
(28(29:31:32:34:35:37:38) sts.)
Cont in dc and sc patt, dec in same way as before at end of next 2(2:3:3:4:4:5:5) RS rows.
(26(27:28:29:30:31:32:33) sts.)
Patt 5(7:5:7:5:7:5:7) rows. Fasten off.
Shape neck. Row 1 (RS) Join yarn in 10th(10th:10th:10th:11th:11th:11th:11th) sc from front edge, 1sc in same sc, 2ch, 1dc in next sc, 2dctog, [1dc in each sc] to end.
(16(17:18:19:19:20:21:22) sts.)
Row 2 1ch, [1sc in each st] to last 2 sts, 2sctog.
Row 3 1sc in first sc, 2ch, 1dc in next sc, 2dctog, [1dc in each sc] to end.

Row 4 As Row 2.
(13(14:15:16:16:17:18:19) sts.)
Patt 4 rows. Fasten off.

SLEEVES

Ribbing Work as given for back ribbing until 27(29:29:31:31:33:33:35) rows have been completed.
Work first and 2nd edging rows as given for back.
(30(32:32:34:34:36:36:38) sts.)
Change to J/10 (6.00mm) hook.
Work 6(4:4:2:2:2:2:2) rows in dc and sc patt as given for back.
Inc row (RS) 1sc in first sc, 2ch, 1dc in next sc, 2dc in foll sc, [1dc in each sc] to last 3sc, 2dc in next sc, 1dc in each of last 2sc.

Cont in dc and sc patt, inc in this way at each end of 3(**4**:4:**3**:3:**0**:0:**0**) foll 6th rows, 2(**1**:1:**1**:3:**8**:8:**7**) foll 4th rows and next 0(**1**:1:**1**:1:**0**:0:**2**) RS rows. *(42(**46**:46:**50**:50:**54**:54:**58**) sts.)* Patt 3(**1**:1:**1**:1:**1**:1:**1**) rows.

Shape top. Next row (RS) Ss in each of first 2(**3**:3:**4**:4:**5**:5:**6**)sc, 1sc in next sc, 2ch, [1dc in each sc] to last 2(**3**:3:**4**:4:**5**:5:**6**)sc, turn. *(38(**40**:40:**42**:42:**44**:44:**46**) sts.)* Cont in dc and sc patt, dec in same way as back at each end of next 1(**2**:2:3:3:**4**:4:**5**) RS rows. *(36 sts.)*
2nd dec row (WS) 2sctog, [1sc in each dc] to last 2 sts, 2sctog. *(34 sts.)*
3rd dec row (RS) 1sc in first st, 2ch, 1dc in next sc, [2dctog] twice, [1dc in each sc] to last 6 sts, [2dctog] twice, 1dc in each of last 2 sts. *(30 sts.)* Work 2nd and 3rd dec rows once more, then work 2nd dec row again. *(22 sts.)*
Fasten off. Weave in ends.

FRONT BANDS

Left front Using H/8 (5.00mm) hook, join yarn at neck edge.
Row 1 Work 95(**98**:98:**101**:104:**107**:107:**110**)sc along front edge.
Row 2 1ch, miss first sc, [1sc around stem of each sc] to end. *(94(**97**:97:**100**:103:**106**:106:**109**) sts.)*
Row 3 1ch, [1sc in each sc] to end **.
Row 3 forms sc. Work 2 more rows sc. Do not turn after last row.
Work 1 row crab st (sc backward).
Fasten off. Weave in ends.
Right front Joining yarn at lower edge, work as given for left front band to **.
Buttonhole row (WS) 1ch, 1sc in each of first 2sc, [2ch, miss 2sc, 1sc in each of next 13(**13**:13:**14**:14:**15**:15:**15**) sc] 4 times, 2ch, miss 2sc, [1sc in each sc] to end.

Next row 1ch, [1sc in each sc and 2sc in each 2ch sp] to end. Do not fasten off. Work 1 row crab st (sc backward).
Fasten off. Weave in ends.

COLLAR

Matching sts, join shoulders. Using 5.00mm (H/8) hook, join yarn in ridge at beg of right front band.
Row 1 Work 23(**23**:23:**23**:24:**24**:24:**24**)sc up right front neck, 24(**24**:24:**24**:26:**26**:26:**26**) sc across back neck and 23(**23**:23:**23**:24:**24**:24:**24**)sc down left front neck ending with last sc in ridge at beg of left front band. *(70(**70**:70:**70**:74:**74**:74:**74**) sc)*
Row 2 1ch, [1sc in each sc] to end. Row 2 forms sc. Change to J/10 (6.00mm) hook. Work 18 more rows sc. Fasten off.
Edging Using H/8 (5.00mm) hook, join yarn in corner of right front band and work 1 row of crab st (sc backward) along row ends of band, row ends of collar, in sc along edge, down row ends of collar and along row ends of band.
Fasten off. Weave in all ends.

TO FINISH

Press according to ball band.
Set in sleeves. Add surface decoration.
Join side and sleeve seams.
Sew on buttons.

SURFACE DECORATION

Diamond panel 1. First line Using J/10 (6.00mm) hook and with RS facing, start above welt in 2nd edging row on right front. Holding yarn underneath front, insert hook between dc and band edging and bring a loop of yarn to RS. Work 1ch over lower part of first dc to the left, 1ch over upper part of foll dc to the left, 3rd ch in sp after next sc in row above to the left, 4th ch

in sp next to dc in row above sc, 5th ch over lower part of dc in row above to the right, 6th ch over upper part of foll dc to the right, 7th ch in sp after next sc in row above to the right and 8th ch in sp between dc in row above sc. Cont in this way working 4 surface ch left and 4 right until neck edge. Fasten off.
2nd line Placing surface chain so that chains share the same hole when they meet and working from right to left, then left to right, work 2nd line in the same way.
Placing pairs of lines so that there are 3dc between widest part of diamonds, work 2 more panels on right front, then work 3 panels on left front.
Surface bobbles Worked up center diamond panel on each front. Using J/10 (6.00mm) hook, with RS facing you and the yarn underneath, join yarn and bring a loop through to one side of sc in center of first outlined area at lower edge. * Work 5ch, take hook to the other side of sc, bring loop up and pull through last ch, lengthen ch and remove hook, insert hook to one side where surface ch of diamonds meet above, bring hook out by loop and tensioning loop so fabric lies flat, pull long ch through on back of work, work 1ch over surface ch at point of diamond, pull up loop and remove hook, insert hook in center of next outlined area, bring hook out by loop and pull long ch through on back of work. Rep from * until all diamonds in the panel have a center 5ch bobble. Fasten off. Weave in all ends.

Textured Cardigan Coat

All you need to make this amazing coat is chain stitch and single crochet. It is worked in one piece to the armholes, then divided and worked straight for back and fronts. The sleeves are almost straight pieces with fold-back cuffs. The yarn shades gently in color, creating a soft, striped effect as you work. Wrap over and pin or belt the coat or add pompoms and leave open.

ESTIMATED TIME TO COMPLETE

The first size coat took 30 hours, including the pompoms.

YARN

Noro Silk Garden (45% silk, 45% mohair, 10% wool) worsted (Aran) weight yarn, approx. 109yd (100m) per 1¾oz (50g) ball
18(**21**) balls in Nagano 522

HOOK AND EQUIPMENT

M/13 (9.00mm) crochet hook

Yarn needle

FINISHED MEASUREMENTS

To fit: bust 34–38(**40–44**)in [86–97(**102–112**)cm]

Actual measurements: bust 45(**50¾**)in [114(**129**)cm]; length 33½(**34¼**)in [85(**87**)cm]; **sleeve** (before folding cuff back) 19in [**48**cm].

Figures in parentheses refer to larger size. One figure refers to all sizes.

GAUGE

8 [1sc, 1ch, 1sc] groups to 6in (15cm), 10 rows to 4in (10cm) over pattern using M/13 (9.00mm) hook. Change hook size if necessary to obtain this gauge.

ABBREVIATIONS

ch = chain; **cont** = continue; **inc** = increase; **patt** = pattern; **rep** = repeat; **RS** = right side; **sc** = single crochet; **ss** = slip stitch; **[ ]** = work instructions in brackets as directed.

TIPS

▪ The hook size is larger than usual for this weight of yarn so the stitch pattern is very open; be sure to check your gauge carefully.

▪ Once you get going, this is definitely a project for cold evenings as the back and fronts will act as a lap blanket! If you want to carry work around, crochet the sleeves.

▪ Pompoms are optional; if you don't want them you'll need one less ball of yarn.

▪ If you prefer to make an blanket or wrap, work as given for back and fronts until about 1½ balls of yarn are left. Finish edges with two rounds of sc in same way as the coat. Use any spare yarn for pompoms.

BACK AND FRONTS

Make 184(**208**)ch loosely.

Row 1 (RS) * Miss 2ch, [**1sc**, 1ch, **1sc**] in next ch, rep from * to last ch, 1sc in last ch. *(61(**69**) groups)*

Row 2 1ch, miss first sc, * [**1sc**, 1ch, **1sc**] in next sc, miss 1ch and 1sc, rep from * to end, 1sc in last ch.
Row 2 forms the patt. Cont in patt, work 58 more rows.

Right front. Next row (RS) 1ch, miss first sc, * [**1sc**, 1ch, **1sc**] in next sc, miss 1ch and 1sc, rep from * 14(**16**) more times, 1sc in next sc, turn and complete right front on these 15(**17**) groups. Patt 23(**25**) more rows. Fasten off.

Back With RS facing, join yarn to 2nd sc of group at right armhole.

Next row (RS) 1ch, * [**1sc**, 1ch, **1sc**] in next sc, miss 1ch and 1sc, rep from * 28(**32**) more times, 1sc in next sc, turn and complete back on these 29(**33**) groups. Patt 23(**25**) more rows. Fasten off.

Left front With RS facing, join yarn in 2nd sc of group at left armhole.

Next row (RS) 1ch, * [**1sc**, 1ch, **1sc**] in next sc, miss 1ch and 1sc, rep from * 14(**16**) more times, 1sc in last ch. Complete left front on these 15(**17**) groups. Patt 23(**25**) more rows. Fasten off. Weave in all ends (see page 119).

SLEEVES

Make 61(**70**)ch loosely.

Work Row 1 as given for back and fronts. 20(**23**) groups.

Cont in patt as given for back and fronts, work 24 rows.

Inc row 1ch, miss first sc, [**1sc**, 1ch, **1sc**] in each of next 3 sc, patt to end, work [**1sc**, 1ch, **1sc**] in last sc, 1sc in last ch. 22(**25**) groups. Patt 11 rows. Work inc row again. 24(**27**) groups. Patt 10 rows. Fasten off. Weave in all ends.

TO FINISH

Press according to ball band. Join 10(**11**) groups of back to each front for shoulders. Join sleeve seams, reversing seams for 12 rows at lower edge for turn back cuffs. Set in sleeves.

Edgings With RS facing, join yarn at lower edge of left front, work 123(**139**) sc along lower edge of left front, back, and right front, work 2 more sc in same place as last sc for corner, work 84(**86**)sc up right front, 3sc in corner, 10(**12**)sc along right front neck edge, 23(**27**)sc across back neck, 10(**12**) sc along left front edge, 3sc in corner and 84(**86**)sc down left front edge, 2sc in same place as first sc, ss in first sc, turn. Working 3sc in each corner sc, work 1 more round of sc. Fasten off. Working 41(**47**)sc on first round, finish lower edges of sleeves in the same way. Turn cuffs back.

Make 15 x 2in (5cm) pompoms (see page 123). Sew 5 along neck edge and 5 on each front.

Pink Flower Top

Although it's made in fingering (4ply) cotton, several tricks make this top fast to finish. Each petal of the flower motif is made up of three double trebles clustered together and worked straight into the starting ring with chain links between petals, so in just one round you will have completed a motif. The motifs are joined as you work to make an open, lacy fabric, so you will see the top grow quickly.

ESTIMATED TIME TO COMPLETE

Making and joining each flower motif, around 6 minutes, and there are 138 motifs in the top plus the edging; total time taken, 15 hours.

YARN

Rowan Summerlite 4 Ply (100% cotton) fingering (4-ply) weight yarn, approx. 191yd (175m) per 1¾oz (50g) ball
4 balls in Pinched Pink 426

HOOK AND EQUIPMENT

C/2(**D/3**) [2.50(**3.00**)mm] crochet hook
Yarn needle

FINISHED MEASUREMENTS

To fit: bust 32-34(**36-38**)in [81-86(**91-97**)cm]

Actual measurements: bust 34½(37¾)in [88(**96**)cm]; **length** 21(**22¾**)in [53(**58**)cm]

Figures in parentheses refer to larger size. One figure refers to both sizes.

GAUGE

Each flower motif measures 2⅛(2⅜)in [5.5(**6**)cm] when pressed, using C/2(**D/3**) [2.50(**3.00**)mm] hook. Change hook size if necessary to obtain these gauges.

ABBREVIATIONS

ch = chain; **cont** = continue; **dtr** = double treble; **3dtrtog** = leaving last loop of each stitch on hook, work 3 double trebles, yoh and pull through 4 loops on hook; **RS** = right side; **sc** = single crochet; **sp(s)** = space(es); **ss** = slip stitch; **st** = stitch; **WS** = wrong side; **yoh** = yarn over hook; **[ ]** = work instructions in brackets as directed.

NOTES

The motifs are joined in rounds for the back and front to the armholes; then motifs and joins are omitted to shape the armholes and neck.

Join the motifs with WS together; RS of the motif you're working on facing you.

BACK AND FRONTS

First line of motifs. First flower motif Wind yarn around finger to form a ring.

Round 1 (RS) 5ch, leaving last loop of each st on hook, work 2dtr in ring, yoh and pull through 3 loops on hook, 7ch, [3dtrtog in ring, 7ch] 5 times, ss in 5th ch. Fasten off. Weave in ends (see page 119).

2nd flower motif Work as First flower motif until 6 petals have been completed, 3ch, 1sc in a 7ch sp of First flower motif, 3ch, ss in 5th ch. Fasten off. Weave in ends.

Cont working motifs, joining each one in the 7ch sp opposite the previous join until a line of 15 motifs has been completed.

16th flower motif Work as First flower motif until 3 petals have been completed, join in 15th motif, work 3 more petals, join in first motif to make a round.

2nd line of motifs. First flower motif Work until 5 petals have been completed, join in 7ch sp to the right of top petal of first motif, work one petal, join in 7ch sp at left of top petal of 2nd motif.

2nd flower motif Work until 4 petals have been completed, join in previous motif, then in 2nd and 3rd motifs of first line of motifs.

Cont joining in this way until 15 motifs have been joined.

16th flower motif Work until 3 petals have been completed, join in 15th motif, last 2 sps of first line and in first motif of 2nd line between each of the last 3 petals.

Cont making and joining motifs in this way until 6 lines of motifs have been completed.

Shape armholes and neck. 7th line of motifs Make and join 7 motifs, miss one motif, [make and join 3 motifs, miss one motif] twice.

Back Cont on 7 motifs, join 8 motifs for 8th line of motifs and 7 motifs for 9th line of motifs.

Left and right fronts Cont on 3 motifs at each side. Placing motifs so neck hole is wider each time, join 3 motifs at each side for 8th line of motifs and 2 motifs at each side for 9th line of motifs. Join fronts to back with 2 motifs at each side.

Neck edging With RS facing, join yarn in 7ch sp of right back neck motif.

Round 1 (RS) 1ch, [7sc in 7ch sp, 4ch, 7sc in next 7ch sp] 4 times, [4ch, 7sc in each of next two 7ch sps] 4 times, [4ch, 7sc in next 7ch sp] twice, [4ch, 7sc in each of next two 7ch sps] 4 times, 4ch.

Round 2 Ss in first sc, [4ch, ss in 1st ch, ss in each of next 2 sc] 3 times, ss in 4ch sp, 4ch, ss in 1st ch, ss in 4ch sp, cont working picots with ss between in this way to end of round, ss in first ss. Fasten off.

Armhole edgings With RS facing, join yarn at underarms and complete to match neck edging.

Lower edging With RS facing, join yarn in sp level with underarm and complete to match neck edging.

TO FINISH
Weave in all ends. Press according to ball band.

Cream Flowered Tunic

This tunic is made from the same easy-to-work-and-join one-round motifs as the Pink Flower Top on page 52, but the longer, looser-fitting simple T-shape gives a very different effect. Wear this over a plain dress for a party or layer it over a sweater for a pretty look on cooler days.

ESTIMATED TIME TO COMPLETE

Each motif took 6 minutes; for the first size tunic 40 hours, including edging.

YARN

DMC Natura Just Cotton (100% cotton) fingering (4-ply) weight yarn, approx. 170yd (155m) per 1¾oz (50g) ball
   8(**10**) balls in Ivory 2

HOOK AND EQUIPMENT

C/2(**D/3**) [2.50(**3.00**)mm] crochet hook

Yarn needle

FINISHED MEASUREMENTS

To fit: bust [32 to 34(**36 to 38**)in] 81 to 86(**91 to 97**)cm

Actual measurements: bust 39(**42½**)in [99(**108**)cm]; **length** 31½(**34½**)in [80(**87.5**)cm]; **sleeve** 17½(**19**)in [44.5(**48.5**)cm]

Figures in parentheses refer to larger sizes. One figure refers to all sizes.

GAUGE

Each motif measures 2⅛(**2⅜**)in [5.5(**6**)cm] using C/2(**D/3**) [2.50(**3.00**)mm] hook. Change hook size if necessary to obtain this size motif.

ABBREVIATIONS

ch = chain; **cont** = continue; **dtr** = double treble; **3dtrtog** = leaving last loop of each st on hook, work 3 dtr, yoh and pull through 4 loops on hook; **rep** = repeat; **RS** = right side; **sc** = single crochet; **sp** = space; **ss** = slip stitch; **st(s)** = stitch(es); **WS** = wrong side; **yoh** = yarn over hook; **[ ]** = work instructions in brackets as directed.

BACK AND FRONT

First line of motifs Work as given for Pink Flower Top (see page 52) until 17 motifs have been completed. Join in a ring with 18th motif in same way as given for 16th motif of Pink Flower Top. Cont making and joining motifs in same way as Pink Flower Top until 11 rounds of motifs have been completed.

Front and sleeves. First line of motifs (RS) Make and join 8 motifs in a row for left sleeve, make and join 9 motifs across front, make and join 8 motifs in a row for right sleeve.

2nd line of motifs With RS facing, make and join 24 motifs.

3rd line of motifs With RS facing, make and join 25 motifs.

Neck shaping. Next line of motifs With RS facing, make and join 10 motifs, omit center 4 motifs, make and join 10 motifs.

Back and sleeves Work back as front until 2nd line of motifs has been completed.

3rd line of motifs Make 10 motifs joining to front and back each time, join next motif to back and one sp of last motif at neck edge, join 3 motifs to back only, join next motif to back and one sp of first motif at neck edge, join last 10 motifs to front and back each time.

JOIN SLEEVES

Left sleeve With WS facing and taking both sides of sleeves together each time, join yarn to 2nd 7ch sp of motifs at cuff edge, * 2sc in sp, 1sc in 3dtrtog, 2sc in next sp, 7ch, rep from * 6 more times, 2sc in sp, 1sc in 3dtrtog, 2sc in next sp. Fasten off.

Underarm motif 5ch, ss in first ch to form a ring, 1ch, 1sc in ring, [* 5ch, 1sc in sc joining motifs, 5ch *, 1sc in ring] 5 times, rep from * to *, ss in first sc. Fasten off.

Right sleeve Join and work underarm motif in same way as left sleeve. Weave in ends (see page 119).

SLEEVE EDGINGS

Fill each space between motifs at cuff edge of sleeves with a half motif made and joined until 4 petals of motif have been completed, work 1dtr in ring, fasten off.

With RS facing, join yarn at sleeve seam.

Round 1 1ch, 2sc in first sp after join, * [1sc in 3dtrtog, 5sc in next sp] twice, 2sc in each of next 2 sps, rep from * 5 times, 1sc in 3dtrtog, 5sc in next sp, 1sc in 3dtrtog, 2sc in last sp, ss in first sc. Fasten off. Weave in ends.

NECK EDGING

With RS facing, join yarn to right-hand 3dtrtog of shoulder motif.

Round 1 1ch, * [1sc in 3dtrtog, 5sc in 7ch sp] once, 1sc in 3dtrtog, 2ch, rep from * around neck edge working instructions in brackets twice across 3 motifs at center back and front, ending ss in first sc.

Round 2 1ch, [1sc in each sc and 2sc in each 2ch sp] to end, ss in first sc. Fasten off.

LOWER EDGING

With RS facing, join yarn to right-hand 3dtrtog of motif at left side. Complete to match neck edging, working instructions in brackets twice for each rep.

TO FINISH

Weave in all ends. Press according to ball band.

TIPS

▓ If you prefer, rather than winding the yarn around your finger you could start each motif with 5ch, then ss in first ch to form a ring. It is a bit easier to work into a chain ring but the centers of the motifs won't be as small.

▓ To fasten off the motifs neatly don't use chain stitch; cut the end and pull it through after working the last stitch, then weave the end in to join the round.

Chapter 3
For the Home

Flowery Paisley Blanket

It's fascinating to see the characteristic paisley shape appear as you work these motifs. The stitches are all straightforward; although the joining can be a bit fiddly, the effect is really worth it. The blanket in the picture is made from 20 paisley blocks with simple filler squares in between. You can adjust the size of your blanket by changing the number of motifs you join together.

ESTIMATED TIME TO COMPLETE

For each motif, 40 minutes; blanket, 24 hours.

YARN

A variety of wool and wool mix light worsted (DK) yarns were used to make this blanket, with an average of 131yd (120m) to a 1¾oz (50g) ball
- 5 x 1¾oz (50g) balls of wool mix light worsted (DK) in shades of cream
- 4 x 1¾oz (50g) balls of same or similar light worsted (DK) in shades of lime and grass green

HOOK AND EQUIPMENT

E/4 (3.50mm) crochet hook

Yarn needle

FINISHED MEASUREMENTS

Width 37¼in (95cm); **length** 41in (104cm)

GAUGE

Each paisley motif measures 4½ x 7½in (11 x 19cm); each joined block measures 7½ x 10½in (19 x 26cm), all when pressed, using E/4 (3.50mm) hook. Change hook size if necessary to obtain this size block.

ABBREVIATIONS

ch = chain; **dc** = double crochet; **sc** = single crochet; **tr** = treble; **rep** = repeat; **RS** = right side; **sp(s)** = space(s); **ss** = slip stitch; **WS** = wrong side; **[ ]** = work instructions in brackets as directed.

NOTES

The instructions do not give color changes; you can make the motifs in any combination of colors that you prefer.

For the effect in the picture, work alternate paisley motifs in shades of lime and grass green sandwiched between cream for the center flowers and outer edging. Use cream for the edging of each motif, and alternate green and cream for the filler squares.

Yarn amounts given are approximate. As with any scrap-yarn project, different light worsted yarns may vary in length-to-weight ratio.

TIPS

- The paisley motifs and the edging that joins them are given separately to make it easier to carry the work around. If you find it easier, just continue with the edging and join motifs as you work them.

- The instructions explain how to join the pieces with crochet; this gives a very neat finish, but if you prefer, you could omit the joins from the last round of the block edging and the filler squares, then sew the pieces together.

- You can use any color scheme you like. Shades of blue or natural work well, or you can use up even the tiniest scraps of leftover yarn by making each paisley and filler square a wild random mix of colors with a dark contrast for the block edging.

- When changing colors, remember to pull through the last part of the last stitch of a round with the new color.

PAISLEY MOTIF

First flower Make 6ch, ss in first ch to form a ring.

Round 1 (RS) 1ch, 8sc in ring, ss in first sc.

Round 2 1ch, 1sc in first sc, 3ch, [1sc in next sc, 3ch] 7 times, ss in first sc. Fasten off.

2nd flower Make 7ch, ss in first ch to form a ring.

Round 1 (RS) 1ch, 10sc in ring, ss in first sc.

Round 2 1ch, 1sc in first sc, 4ch, [1sc in next sc, 4ch] 7 times, 1sc in next sc, 2ch, 1sc in a 3ch sp of first flower, 2ch, 1sc in next sc, 2ch, 1sc in next 3ch sp of first flower, 2ch, ss in first sc. Fasten off.

Border Join yarn in first flower in 3rd sp before join.

Round 1 (RS) 1ch, 1sc in same sp as join, [2ch, 1sc in next sp] twice, 2ch, 1dc in sp with join, 2ch, now work around 2nd flower, 1tr in next sp with join, [2ch, 1sc in next sp] 8 times, 2ch, 1tr in sp with join, 2ch, 1dc in sp with join on first flower, [2ch, 1sc in next sp] 3 times, 2ch, ss in first sc, make 15ch, do not turn.

Round 2 2sc in 2nd ch from hook, [1sc in next ch, 2sc in foll ch] 4 times, 1sc in each of next 4ch, 1sc in same place as ss, [2sc in next sp, 1sc in next st] 17 times, 1sc in last sp, ss in lower loop of each of first 3ch, turn.

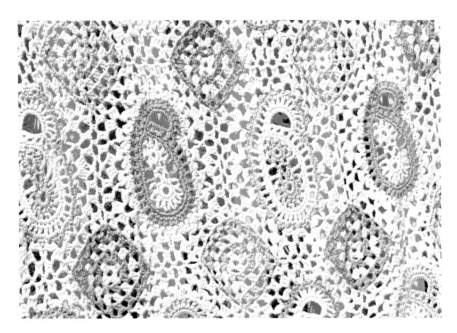

Round 3 (WS) 1ch, 1dc in first sc, [1ch, miss 1sc, 1dc in next sc] 11 times, [1ch, 1dc in next sc] 9 times, [1ch, miss 1sc, 1dc in next sc] 13 times, [1ch, 1dc in next sc] 10 times, 1ch, miss 1sc, 1dc in next sc, place RS together to work 1sc in 5th sp from beginning of this round, ss in next dc, ss in next sp, insert hook in end ch of Round 1 and ss to next st. Fasten off. With RS facing, join yarn in sp made when joining end ch to 3rd round.
Round 4 1ch, 1sc in same sp as join, [1sc, 3ch, 1sc] in each of next 39 sps, 1sc in last free sp, 1ch, 1sc in first 3ch sp, 1ch, 1sc in same place as sc in last free sp, 1sc in sp made with joined ch, ss in first sc. 40 3ch sps. Fasten off. Make 19 more paisley motifs.

EDGE AND JOIN MOTIFS

1st block With RS facing, join yarn in sp to the left of the two joined sps in the crook of the paisley.
Round 1 1sc in same sp as join, 5ch, [miss 1sp, 5sc in next sp, 5ch] 19 times, 4sc in first sp, ss in first sc.

Round 2 1sc in 5ch sp, 2ch, 2dc in same sp, 3ch, 3dc in same sp, * 3ch, 1sc in next sp, 3ch, [3dc, 3ch, 3dc] in foll sp, rep from * 8 more times, 3ch, 1sc in next sp, 1ch, 1dc in 2nd ch.
Round 3 1sc in dc sp, 2ch, 1dc in dc sp, * 2ch, [2dc, 2ch, 2dc] in next sp, [2ch, 2dc in foll sp] twice, rep from * 3 times, 2ch, 2sc in next sp, 2ch, ** [2dc in next sp, 2ch] twice, [2dc, 2ch, 2dc] in foll sp, 2ch, rep from ** 3 times, [2dc in next sp, 2ch] twice, 2sc in foll sp, 2ch, 2dc in next sp, 2ch, ss in 2nd ch. Fasten off.
2nd Block Work as first block, joining 3rd round to 8 sps of first long side on the right of first motif by working 1ch, 1sc in adjacent sp, 1ch, between dc groups instead of 2ch.
Edge and join 3rd motif to 2nd motif, 4th motif to 3rd motif and 5th motif to 4th motif in the same way. Join 6th motif to top edge of 1st motif, 7th motif to side edge of 6th motif and top edge of 2nd motif, 8th motif to 7th and 3rd motifs, 9th motif to 8th and 4th motifs and 10th motif to 9th and 5th motifs. Edge and join two more lines of 5 paisley motifs in the same way.

FILLER SQUARE

Make 8ch, ss in first ch to form a ring.
Round 1 (RS) 1sc in ring, 5ch, [2dc in ring, 3ch] 3 times, 1dc in ring, ss in 2nd ch.
Round 2 1sc in first 3ch sp, 5ch, 2dc in same 3ch sp, [2ch, 2dc in next 3ch sp, 3ch, 2dc in same 3ch sp] 3 times, 2ch, 1dc in first 3ch sp, ss in 2nd ch.
Round 3 1sc in first 3ch sp, 5ch, 2dc in same 3ch sp, [2ch, 2dc in next 2ch sp, 2ch, 2dc in next 3ch sp, 3ch, 2dc in same 3ch sp] 3 times, 2ch, 2dc in next 2ch sp, 2ch, 1dc in first 3ch sp, ss in 2nd ch.
Join square in space between blocks.
Round 4 1sc in first 3ch sp, 3ch, 1sc in top right corner sp of first block, 1ch, 1sc in corner sp of 2nd block, 1ch, 2dc in first 3ch sp of square, * [1ch, 1sc in next sp of block edge, 1ch, 2dc in next sp of square] 3 times, 1ch, 1sc in corner sp of 2nd block, 1ch, 1dc in corner sp of next block, 1ch, 2dc in same sp of square as last 2dc, rep from * 2 more times, [1ch, 1sc in next sp of block edge, 1ch, 2dc in next sp of square] twice, 1ch, 1sc in next sp of block edge, 1ch, 1dc in first 3ch sp of square, ss in 2nd ch. Fasten off. Make and join 11 more filler squares.

TO FINISH

Weave in ends (see page 119). Press.

Cozy Creamy Blanket

The only stitches you need to know to work this blanket are chain stitch, slip stitch, and double crochet. The squares are a simple variation on a traditional block with bobbles, made by clustering double crochets together, adding texture. This is an ideal project to carry around; although the squares are large, there are just six rounds to work, so you can continue your project whenever you have a few spare moments.

ESTIMATED TIME TO COMPLETE

Each square, 25 minutes; 5 hours for 12 blocks, plus 2 hours to join the blocks and edge the blanket. Total time, 7 hours.

YARN

Debbie Bliss Dulcie (47% cotton, 47% acrylic, 6% nylon) bulky (chunky) weight yarn, approx. 82yd (75m) per 1¾oz (50g) ball
    14 balls in Ecru 02

HOOKS AND EQUIPMENT

K/10½ (7.00mm) and J/10 (6.00mm) crochet hooks

Yarn needle

FINISHED MEASUREMENTS

Width 34¼in (87cm); **length** 45¼in (115cm)

GAUGE

Each square measures 10 x 10in (25 x 25cm) using K/10½ (7.00mm) hook. Change hook size if necessary to obtain this size square.

ABBREVIATIONS

ch = chain; **dc** = double crochet; **4dcCl** = leaving last loop of each on hook, work 4dc all in same st or sp as directed, yoh and pull through 5 loops on hook; **rep** = repeat; **RS** = right side; **sp** = space; **ss** = slip stitch; **st(s)** = stitch(es); **yoh** = yarn over hook; **[ ]** = work instructions in brackets as directed.

NOTES

One ball of yarn will make two squares with some left over. If you want to avoid weaving in ends while working a square, put this yarn aside until the end and use it to join the squares and edge the blanket.

Working into a ring of thread rather than a starting chain gives a neat center. If you weave the starting end between each of the 3ch, you can work over it in the next round and just snip the end off. Otherwise you must weave it in very securely.

TIPS

- If you weave in ends or work over them as you go, there's no making up to do!

- Big hooks make for fast work, but they can be clumsy to handle; make sure you turn the hook slightly as you pull loops through so you don't catch or split the yarn.

- The trick with yarn this thick is to be sure to handle it gently. Make the stitches with a smooth, turning action; don't snatch them through or your gauge could be too tight.

- If you want to check your gauge before completing the square, each round should be approximately ⅞in (2cm) high.

- If you want a bigger blanket, just work out how many squares you need, allowing 1in (3cm) for each join. Add 1 ball of yarn for every 2 extra squares.

BOBBLE SQUARE

Using K/10½ (7.00mm) hook, wrap yarn around finger to form a ring.

Round 1 3ch, 11dc in ring, pull end to tighten ring, ss in 3rd ch. *(12 sts.)*

Round 2 3ch, leaving last loop of each st on hook, work 3dc in same place as ss, yoh and pull through 4 loops on hook, [1ch, 4dcCl in next dc] twice, 5ch, * [4dcCl in next dc, 1ch] 3 times, work 4 more ch, rep from * twice, ss in 3rd ch.

Round 3 Ss in first 1ch sp, 3ch, leaving last loop of each st on hook, work 3dc in same place as ss, yoh and pull through 4 loops on hook, 1ch, 4dcCl in next 1ch sp, * 2ch, [2dc, 2ch] twice in 5ch sp, 4dcCl in next 1ch sp, 1ch, 4dcCl in next 1ch sp, rep from * twice, 2ch, [2dc, 2ch] twice in 5ch sp, ss in 3rd ch.

Round 4 Ss in first 1ch sp, 3ch, leaving last loop of each st on hook, work 3dc in same place as ss, yoh and pull through 4 loops on hook, 2ch, * 1dc in 2ch sp, 1dc in each of next 2dc, [1dc, 2ch, 1dc] in next 2ch sp, 1dc in each of next 2dc, 1dc in foll 2ch sp, 2ch, 4dcCl in next 1ch sp, 2ch, rep from * twice, 1dc in next 2ch sp, 1dc in each of next 2dc, [1dc, 2ch, 1dc] in foll 2ch sp, 1dc in each of next 2dc, 1dc in last 2ch sp, 2ch, ss in 3rd ch.

Round 5 3ch, [2dc in 2ch sp, 1dc in each of next 4dc, 2ch, 4dcCl in 2ch sp, 2ch, 1dc in each of next 4dc, 2dc in 2ch sp, 1dc in 4dcCl] 4 times, omitting last dc, ss in 3rd ch.

Round 6 3ch, 1dc in each of next 6dc, * 2ch, [4dcCl in next 2ch sp, 2ch] twice, 1dc in each of next 13dc, rep from * twice, 2ch, [4dcCl in next 2ch sp, 2ch] twice, 1dc in each of next 6dc, ss in 3rd ch.

Fasten off. Weave in ends (see page 119).

Make 12 bobble squares.

JOIN SQUARES

Using J/10 (6.00mm) hook, join yarn in corner 2ch sp. With WS together and square with joined yarn in front, join along one edge of two squares by working 2ch, 1sc in corner space of back square, 2ch, 1sc in next 2ch sp of front square, 2ch, 1sc in next 2ch sp of back square, 2ch, miss 1dc, 1sc in next dc of front square, 2ch miss 1dc, 1sc in next dc of back square, continue in this way working into alternate dc, then into spaces at end. Fasten off. Join edges of squares in this way to make the blanket 3 squares by 4 squares.

Filler motifs Work one in each space between joins at corners of squares. Wind yarn around finger to make a ring.

Round 1 (RS) 1ch, 1sc in ring, 1dc in corner sp of first square, [1sc in ring, 1dc in corner sp of next square] 3 times, pull end to tighten ring, ss in 1st sc. Fasten off. Weave in all ends.

Edging Using K/10½ (7.00mm) hook and with RS facing, join yarn in a 2ch sp along one edge.

Round 1 Working 2sc in each sp along edge, 1sc in each dc, and 5sc in each corner sp, work one round of sc, ss in first sc, turn.

Round 2 Working 1sc in each sc and 3sc in corner sc, work one round sc, ss in first sc.

Fasten off. Weave in all ends.

Irish Lace Pillow

Raised flowers and picot mesh make a delicate design, but this pillow is easier than it looks. The front is made from just four motifs joined to make a square, with an extra flower sewn on in the center. And there are no complicated stitches, just the basics: chain, slip stitch, single crochet, half double crochet and double crochet, combined to create a stunning, decorative effect.

ESTIMATED TIME TO COMPLETE

The pillow front took 7 hours.

YARN AND MATERIALS

DMC Natura Just Cotton (100% cotton) fingering (4-ply) weight yarn, approx. 170yd (155m) per 1¾oz (50g) ball
2 balls in Sable 3
12 x 12in (30 x 30cm) pillow form with cover

HOOK AND EQUIPMENT

C/2 (2.50mm) crochet hook
Yarn needle

FINISHED MEASUREMENTS

Width 12in (30cm); **length** 12in (30cm)

GAUGE

Each 11-round motif measures 5½ x 5½in (14 x 14cm), when pressed, using C/2 (2.50mm) hook. Change hook size if necessary to obtain this size motif.

ABBREVIATIONS

ch = chain; **dc** = double crochet; **hdc** = half double crochet; **picot** = 3ch, 1sc in 3rd ch from hook; **rep** = repeat; **RS** = right side; **sc** = single crochet; **sp(s)** = space(s); **ss** = slip stitch; **st(s)** = stitch(es); **[ ]** = work instructions in brackets as directed.

NOTE

It saves a lot of counting back along the chain if you move your finger and thumb up to grip the chain before working the picot, because you can see immediately which chain to work the sc into.

TIPS

■ If you weave in ends or work over them as you go, there's no making up to do!

■ Big hooks make for fast work, but they can be clumsy to handle; make sure you turn the hook slightly as you pull loops through so you don't catch or split the yarn.

■ The trick with yarn this thick is to be sure to handle it gently. Make the stitches with a smooth, turning action; don't snatch them through or your gauge could be too tight.

■ If you want to check your gauge before completing the square, each round should be approximately ⅞in (2cm) high.

LACY MOTIF

Make 6ch, ss in first ch to form a ring.

Round 1 (RS) 1ch, 12sc in ring, ss in first sc.

Round 2 1ch, 1sc in same place as ss, 4ch, [miss 1sc, 1sc in next sc, 4ch] 5 times, miss 1sc, ss in first sc.

Round 3 [1sc, 1hdc, 3dc, 1hdc, 1sc] in each 4ch sp, ss in first sc.

Round 4 Taking hook behind petals, work 1sc around the stem of first sc of Round 2, 5ch, [1sc around stem of next sc of Round 2, 5ch] 5 times, ss in first sc.

Round 5 [1sc, 1hdc, 5dc, 1hdc, 1sc] in each 5ch sp, ss in first sc.

Round 6 Taking hook behind petals, work 1sc around the stem of first sc of Round 4, 7ch, [1sc around stem of next sc of Round 4, 7ch] 5 times, ss in first sc.

Round 7 [1sc, 1hdc, 7dc, 1hdc, 1sc] in each 7ch sp, ss in first sc.

Round 8 Taking hook behind petals, work 1sc around the stem of first sc of Round 6, 9ch, [1sc around stem of next sc of Round 6, 9ch] 5 times, ss in first sc.

Round 9 [* 1sc, 1ch, 1picot, 2ch, 1picot *, 2ch, 1sc] twice in each of first five 9ch sps and once in last 9ch sp, rep from * to * in last 9ch sp, 1dc in first sc, turn, ss in each of next 2ch, turn.

Round 10 1ch, 1sc between picots in first sp, * 8ch, 1sc between picots in next sp, turn, 1sc in sc, 2ch, 9dc in 8ch sp, 1dc in sc, turn, 1sc in first dc, 3ch, [miss 1dc, 1dc in next dc, 1ch] 4 times, work 2 more ch, ss in next ch and in each of next 2 sts, 1sc in sp between picots, [1ch, 1picot, 2ch, 1picot, 2ch, 1sc between picots in next sp] twice, rep from * 3 more times, omitting last 2ch and 1sc, 1dc in first sc, turn, ss in each of next 2 sts, turn.

Round 11 1sc between picots, * 1ch, 1picot, 2ch, 1picot, 2ch, 1sc in next sp, missping alternate sps across corner motifs, rep from * to end, omitting last 2ch and 1sc, 1dc in first sc. Fasten off. Weave in ends.
Make 3 more lacy motifs.

JOIN MOTIFS

With RS facing, place the first motif at lower right, 2nd motif at top right, 3rd motif at lower left and 4th motif at top left to form a square with 2 picot loops of each motif to the center. Join yarn in 2nd corner sp on the right edge of first motif. With wrong sides together, hold 2nd motif behind first motif.

Joining row (RS) 1ch, 1sc in same sp as join, * 2ch, 1picot, 2ch, 1sc in corresponding sp of 2nd motif, rep from * working alternately into following sps of first and 2nd motifs until 5 sps of each motif have been joined, 10ch, 1sc in 2nd corner sp at right edge of 3rd motif, join 3rd and 4th motifs in same way as first and 2nd motifs. Fasten off. Join across between motifs in the same way.

Center flower Work as given for first 7 rounds of lacy motif. Fasten off. Weave in all ends.

EDGING

With RS facing, join yarn in first of the two sps at one corner.

Round 1 1ch, 1sc in same sp as join, [5ch, 1sc in next sp] to last sp, 5ch, ss in first sc.

Round 2 1ch, [9sc in corner sp, 5sc in each of next 12 sps] 4 times, ss in first sc.

Round 3 1ch, 1sc in each sc, ss in first sc.

Round 4 3ch, [1picot, miss 1sc, 1dc in next sc] to last sc, 1 picot, miss last sc, ss in 3rd ch.
Fasten off. Weave in ends.

TO FINISH

Press according to ball band. Weave in ends. Sew on center flower. Sew pillow front to pillow.

Lace Edge Tablecloth

This delicate fan edging is created with the simplest of stitches. Although the instructions explain how to edge the tablecloth shown in the picture, the edging is very adaptable. You can work it directly into the fabric or make a separate length and sew it on. You can also change the size of the edging according to the yarn you choose; this tablecloth edging is in a firm fingering (4-ply) cotton yarn. In a finer yarn the edging would make a lovely lingerie trim; in a heavier yarn it would suit a shade or a bedspread.

ESTIMATED TIME TO COMPLETE

For the edging, 7 hours.

YARN AND MATERIALS

DMC Natura Just Cotton (100% cotton) fingering (4-ply) weight yarn, approx. 170yd (155m) per 1¾oz (50g) ball
   2 balls in Nacar 35

36½ x 36½in (93 x 93cm) even-weave linen fabric in cream

FINISHED MEASUREMENTS

Width 38in (96.5cm); **length** 38in (96.5cm)

HOOK AND EQUIPMENT

2.00mm (B/1) crochet hook

Yarn needle

GAUGE

Edging is 1in (2.5cm) deep; 2 repeats measure 2½in (6cm) using B/1 (2.00mm) hook. Change hook size if necessary to obtain this gauge.

ABBREVIATIONS

ch = chain; **dc** = double crochet; **foll** = following; **rep** = repeat; **sc** = single crochet; **sp** = space; **ss** = slip stitch; **st(s)** = stitch(es); [ ] = work instructions in brackets as directed.

TIPS

- Make a test piece to be sure that your edging lies flat when made in the fabric and yarn you've chosen.

- To work the sc row evenly along each edge, place markers to divide each edge into 4. Work 58sc to first marker, 1sc in marker place, remove marker, repeat along edge to corner, work 3sc in corner, then continue in the same way around the tablecloth.

- You can make the edging fit around a smaller or larger cloth; just allow about 1¼in (3cm) more or less fabric for each repeat of the edging and make sure that you work a multiple of 8 plus 3 along each edge and 3 from each corner on Round 1.

- To work a straight edging in a ring, without corners, make a number of chain divisible by 8 and ss in first ch. Make the chain loosely, or your edging may not stretch to fit. Work Round 1 into the chain; on following rounds repeat instructions in brackets to omit corners.

- Check out lace maker's supplies if you prefer to edge your linen tablecloth with linen thread.

- If you're trimming a cotton cloth, work the edging separately and sew it on, because it's not always easy to draw threads in very tightly woven cotton fabric.

TABLECLOTH

Preparation Pull threads along each edge of the linen to make sure that the fabric is square. Trim if necessary. Pull out 4 threads 18 threads in from each edge. Fold fabric twice along each edge to make a narrow hem that lines up with space left by drawing the threads. Press the hems.

EDGING

Join yarn in approximately 5 threads from a corner space.

Round 1 Inserting hook in gap left by drawing threads to work over hem, work [235sc evenly along edge and 3sc in corner] 4 times, ss in first sc.

Round 2 1ch, 1sc in same place as ss, * [2ch, miss 1sc, 1sc in next sc, miss 2sc, 5dc in next sc, miss 2sc, 1sc in next sc] 29 times, 2ch, miss 1sc, 1sc in next sc, miss 1sc, 5dc in corner sc, miss 1sc, 1sc in next sc, rep from * 3 more times, omitting last sc and ending ss in first sc.

Round 3 Ss in first sp, 1ch, 1sc in first sp, * 1ch, [1dc in next dc, 1ch] 5 times, 1sc in next sp, rep from * to end, omitting last sc, ending ss in first sc.

Round 4 Ss in each of first ch and dc, 5ch, [1dc in next dc, 2ch] 3 times, 1dc in foll dc, * [1dc in next dc, 2ch] 4 times, 1dc in foll dc, rep from * to end, ss in 3rd ch. Fasten off. Weave in ends.

TO FINISH

Spray with starch and press.

Comfy Round Pillow

A simple progression of increases makes this circular pillow lie flat. The stitch pattern is just alternate rounds of double and single crochet; for the ridged side just work around the stem instead of into the stitches of the previous round.

ESTIMATED TIME TO COMPLETE

The pillow took 5 hours.

YARN AND MATERIALS

Debbie Bliss Cotton DK (100% cotton) light worsted (DK) weight yarn, approx. 92yd (84m) per 1¾oz (50g) ball
   6 balls in Duck Egg 9
Round pillow form 15in (38cm) diameter
   x 2in (5cm) deep

HOOK AND EQUIPMENT

F/5 (4.00mm) crochet hook
Yarn needle

FINISHED MEASUREMENTS

Diameter 15in (38cm); **depth** 2in (5cm)

GAUGE

18 rounds in patt measure 15in (38cm); 8 rounds sc measure 2in (5cm) using F/5 (4.00mm) hook. Change hook size if necessary to obtain this gauge.

ABBREVIATIONS

alt = alternative; **cont** = continue; **ch** = chain; **dc** = double crochet; **foll** = following; **sc** = single crochet; **ss** = slip st; **st(s)** = stitch(es); [ ] = work instructions in brackets as directed.

TIPS

- Rotate the hook to show the nubbly side of the turning chain; this will help blend it in with the double stitches.

- To help hide the joins in the rounds, instead of working the ss in the usual way, remove the hook and insert it from the back into the 3rd ch or sc, then catch the loop and pull it through. This is particularly good for joining the sc-around-the-post rounds. after the next round, don't cut the yarn; carry it up on the back of the work until needed.

- You can save time at the end by weaving in or working over the ends as you go.

PILLOW

Ridged side Wind yarn around finger to form a ring.

Round 1 3ch, 11dc in ring, pull end to tighten ring, ss in 3rd ch. *(12 sts.)*

Round 2 and every alt round 1ch, 1sc around the stem of each st, ss in first sc.

Round 3 3ch, 1dc in same place as ss, [2dc in each sc] to end, ss in 3rd ch. *(24 sts.)*

Round 5 As Round 3. *(48 sts.)*

Round 7 3ch, 1dc in same place as ss, 1dc in next sc, [2dc in foll sc, 1dc in next sc] to end, ss in 3rd ch. *(72 sts.)*

Round 9 3ch, 1dc in same place as ss, 1dc in each of next 2sc, [2dc in foll sc, 1dc in each of next 2sc] to end, ss in 3rd ch. *(96 sts.)*

Round 11 3ch, 1dc in same place as ss, 1dc in each of next 3sc, [2dc in foll sc, 1dc in each of next 3sc] to end, ss in 3rd ch. *(120 sts.)*

Round 13 3ch, 1dc in same place as ss, 1dc in each of next 4sc, [2dc in foll sc, 1dc in each of next 4sc] to end, ss in 3rd ch. *(144 sts.)*

Round 15 3ch, 1dc in same place as ss, 1dc in each of next 5sc, [2dc in foll sc, 1dc in each of next 5sc] to end, ss in 3rd ch. *(168 sts.)*

Round 17 3ch, 1dc in same place as ss, 1dc in each of next 6sc, [2dc in foll sc, 1dc in each of next 6sc] to end, ss in 3rd ch. *(192 sts.)*

Round 18 As Round 2.
Cont in sc worked in the usual way for 8 more rounds. Fasten off.

Smooth side Work as given for ridged side but working sc rounds in sts in the usual way until 18 rounds have been completed.

TO FINISH

Weave in ends (see page 119). Press according to ball band. Inserting pillow form, taking 1 st from each side together each time, join the two sides of the pillow with a round of sc.

Chapter 4
Babies & Children

Rosebud Hairband

You can use these versatile flowers to decorate almost anything. The flowers are just simple loops of chain so they're quick and easy to make. The leaves take a few more stitches, but they're just as simple. Put them together, and the effect is vibrant and playful.

ESTIMATED TIME TO COMPLETE

Each flower took 10 minutes; hairband took 1 hour 20 minutes.

YARN AND MATERIALS

Small amounts of soft embroidery cotton or fingering (4-ply) cotton yarn in 3 shades of pink (A) and 2 shades of green (B). (The type of yarn you choose to make these flowers and leaves will affect the size and character of the motifs. The flowers in the picture are in soft embroidery cotton that has 11yd (10m) to a ¼oz (5g) hank, the equivalent of a fingering (4-ply) cotton yarn.)

Plain black hairband

Black sewing thread

FINISHED MEASUREMENTS

Each flower 1¼in (3cm); **headband** (from end to end) 14½in (37cm)

HOOK AND EQUIPMENT

C/2 (2.50mm) crochet hook

Sharp needle

GAUGE

Each flower measures 1¼in (3cm) across using C/2 (2.50mm) hook. Change hook size if necessary to obtain this size flower.

ABBREVIATIONS

ch = chain; ; **hdc** = half double crochet; **RS** = right side; **sc** = single crochet; **sp** = space; **ss** = slip st; **st** = stitch; **[ ]** = work instructions in brackets as directed.

NOTE

Use one shade of green for all the centers and the other shade of green for the leaves. Vary the order in which you use the different shades of pink for the petals.

TIPS

- If you don't have the right color yarns in your stash, buy hanks of soft embroidery cotton.

- You can easily use a different size, width, or color headband; simply vary the numbers of flowers you make to decorate it.

- You could also use the flowers and leaves to decorate a bracelet or to make a corsage.

FLOWER

Using first shade of B, wind yarn around finger to make a ring.

Round 1 (RS) 1ch, 10sc in ring, pull end to close ring, change to a shade of A, ss in first sc. Cont in first shade of A.

Round 2 1ch, 1sc in same sc as ss, 2ch, miss 1sc, [1sc in next sc, 2ch, miss 1sc] 4 times, ss in first sc.

Round 3 [Ss in next sp, 5ch, ss in same sp] 5 times. Fasten off.
Join 2nd shade of A in a 2ch sp of 2nd round, behind a 5ch loop of 3rd round and between the 2 ss.

Round 4 1ch, 1sc in same sp, [5ch, 1sc in between ss in next sp] 4 times, 5ch, ss in first sc. Fasten off. Weave in all ends.
Varying the shades of A, make 4 more flowers.

LEAF

Using 2nd shade of B, make 9ch.

Row 1 Ss in 2nd ch from hook, 1sc in each of next 6ch, 3sc in end ch, 1sc in base of next 6ch, turn.

Row 2 Miss first sc, ss in next sc, 1sc in foll sc, 1hdc in each of next 5sc, 3hdc in foll sc, 1hdc in each of next 5sc, ss in foll sc, turn.

Row 3 Ss in first st, [3ch, ss in next st] 12 times. Fasten off. Weave in all ends. Make another leaf.

TO FINISH

Sew the flowers on top of the hairband. Pinch the leaves to make them curl slightly, and sew one leaf at each side.

Chevron Cardigan

This jazzy little cardigan has a sweet flared shape and bell sleeves. The wavy chevron pattern is in double crochet, making it grow quickly. The fronts and back are worked in one up to the armholes, so you don't need to worry about matching the stripes and every row of the shaping that flares the body and sleeves is given; mark them as you work to keep your place.

ESTIMATED TIME TO COMPLETE

The cardigan took 10 hours.

YARN AND MATERIALS

The cardigan is made from a variety of smooth wool mix light worsted (DK) yarns with around 131yd (120m) to a 1¾oz (50g) ball

5¼oz (150g) of wool mix light worsted (DK) in lime green (A)

3oz (75g) of wool mix light worsted (DK) in shades of pink (B)

3oz (75g) of wool mix light worsted (DK) in shades of orange (C)

5 buttons

SIZE AND FINISHED MEASUREMENTS

To fit: age 1 to 2 years; **chest** 20 to 22in (50 to 55cm)

Actual measurements: chest 22¾in (58cm); **length** 14¼in (36cm); **sleeve** 10in (25.5cm)

HOOK AND EQUIPMENT

E/4 (3.50mm) crochet hook

Yarn needle

GAUGE

18 sts and 8½ rows to 4in (10cm) over chevron patt using E/4 (3.50mm) hook. Change hook size if necessary to obtain this gauge.

ABBREVIATIONS

alt = alternate; **beg** = beginning; **ch** = chain; **cont** = continue; **dc** = double crochet; **hdc** = half double crochet; **patt** = pattern; **rep** = repeat; **RS** = right side; **sc** = single crochet; **st(s)** = stitch(es); **tr** = treble; **[ ]** = work instructions in brackets as directed.

NOTES

Yarn amounts are approximate because the light worsted (DK) yarns you use may be a different fiber mix and have a different length to the weight of the yarn.

Make the starting chain very loosely. If necessary use a larger hook.

To work in the same way as the colors shown in the picture, use one shade of lime green but vary the shades of pink and orange.

You can change color for every row or ignore the stripes and work the cardigan all in one color, in which case you'll need approximately 9oz (250g) of wool mix yarn.

TIPS

▨ For the neatest finish at the front edges, break off the yarn at the end of each color stripe and weave in the ends after working the edging.

▨ Choose yarns that can be washed and pressed in the same way. Always follow the care code for the most delicate of the yarns you've used.

▨ If you work in an alternating stripe pattern, it's easy to tell the difference between the right and wrong sides, even though the pattern looks the same, because all rows in A are right-side rows.

▨ Mark every row of shaping on body and sleeves to keep your place easily.

BACK AND FRONTS

Using A, make 142ch loosely.

Row 1 1sc in 2nd ch from hook, [1sc in each ch] to end. *(141 sts.)*

Row 2 (RS) 1sc in first sc, 2ch, [2dc in next sc, 1dc in each of next 2sc, miss 1sc, 1dc in next sc, miss 1sc, 1dc in each of next 2sc, 2dc in foll sc, 1dc in next sc] 14 times.
Change to B.

Row 3 1sc in first dc, 2ch, [2dc in next dc, 1dc in each of next 2dc, miss 1dc, 1dc in next dc, miss 1dc, 1dc in each of next 2dc, 2dc in foll dc, 1dc in next dc] 14 times. Row 3 forms the chevron patt. Cont in chevron patt, working alt stripes of 1 row A, 1 row C, 1 row A, 1 row B, for 8 more rows, ending with a row in B.

Shape sides. Row 1 (RS) Using A, patt 30, ending with 2dc in same dc, * 1dc in each of next 4dc, miss 1dc, 1dc in next dc, miss 1dc, 1dc in each of next 4dc *, beg 2dc in same dc, patt 59, ending 2dc in same dc, rep from * to *, patt 30. *(137 sts.)*

Row 2 Using C, patt 30, * 1dc in each of next 3dc, miss 1dc, 1dc in next dc, miss 1dc, 1dc in each of next 3dc *, patt 59, rep from * to *, patt 30. *(133 sts.)*

Row 3 Using A, patt 30, * 1dc in each of next 2dc, miss 1dc, 1dc in next dc, miss 1dc, 1dc in each of next 2dc *, patt 59, rep from * to *, patt 30. *(129 sts.)*

Row 4 Using B, patt 30, * [1dc in next dc, miss 1dc] twice, 1dc in next dc *, patt 59, rep from * to *, patt 30. *(125 sts.)*

Row 5 Using A, patt 30, * miss 1dc, 1dc in next dc, miss 1dc *, patt 59, rep from * to *, patt 30. *(121 sts.)*

Row 6 Using C, patt 26, * miss 1dc, 1dc in next dc, 2dc in foll dc, miss 1dc, 1dc in next dc, miss 1dc, 2dc in next dc, 1dc in foll dc, miss 1dc *, patt 51, rep from * to *, patt 26. *(117 sts.)*

Row 7 Using A, patt 26, * miss 1dc, 2dc in next dc, miss 1dc, 1dc in next dc, miss 1dc, 2dc in next dc, miss 1dc *, patt 51, rep from * to *, patt 26. *(113 sts.)*

Row 8 Using B, patt 26, * miss 1dc, 1dc in each of next 3dc, miss 1dc *, patt 51, rep from * to *, patt 26. *(109 sts.)*

Row 9 Using A, patt 26, * miss 1dc, 1dc in next dc, miss 1dc *, patt 51, rep from * to *, patt 26. *(105 sts.)*

Row 10 Using C, patt 26, mlss 1dc, patt 51, miss 1dc, patt 26. *(103 sts.)*

Right front. Next row (RS) Using A, patt 26, turn and complete right front on these sts. Cont in chevron stripe patt, work 5 rows. Fasten off.

Shape neck. Next row (RS) Join A in 11th st from front edge, 1sc in same place as join, 2ch, patt to end. *(16 sts.)* Cont in stripe patt, work 4 more rows. Fasten off.

Back With RS facing, join A in next free st.

Row 1 1sc in same place as join, 2ch, patt 50 more sts, turn and complete back on these 51 sts. Patt 9 rows, ending with 1 row less than front to shoulder. Fasten off.

Left front. Row 1 With RS facing, join A in next free st, 1sc in same place as join, 2ch, patt to end. *(26 sts.)* Cont in chevron stripe patt, work 5 rows.

Shape neck. Next row Patt 16, turn. Cont on these 16 sts, work 4 more rows. Fasten off. Weave in all ends (see page 119).

SLEEVES

Using A, make 42ch loosely.
Work Row 1 as given for back and fronts. *(41 sts.)*
Cont in chevron stripe patt as given for back and fronts, work 8 rows.

First dec row (RS) Using A, 1sc in first dc, 2ch, 1dc in each of next 3dc, miss 1dc, 1dc in next dc, patt to last 5 sts, miss 1dc, 1dc in each of next 3dc, 1dc in 2nd ch. *(39 sts.)*

Next row Using B, 1sc in first dc, 2ch, 2dc in next dc, 1dc in foll dc, miss 1dc, patt to last 4 sts, miss 1dc, 1dc in next dc, 2dc in foll dc, 1dc in 2nd ch.

2nd dec row Using A, 1sc in first dc, 2ch, 1dc in each of next 2dc, miss 1dc, 1dc in next dc, patt to last 4 sts, miss 1dc, 1dc in each of next 2dc, 1dc in 2nd ch. *(37 sts.)*

Next row Using C, 1sc in first dc, 2ch, 2dc in next dc, miss 1dc, 1dc in next dc, patt to last 3 sts, miss 1dc, 2dc in next dc, 1dc in 2nd ch.

3rd dec row Using A, 1sc in first dc, 2ch, 1dc in next dc, miss 1dc, 1dc in next dc, patt to last 3 sts, miss 1dc, 1dc in next dc, 1dc in 2nd ch. *(35 sts.)*

Next row Using B, 1sc in first dc, 2ch, 1dc in same place as sc, miss 1dc, 1dc in next dc, patt to last 2 sts, miss 1dc, 2dc in 2nd ch.

4th dec row Using A, 1sc in first dc, 2ch, miss 1dc, 1dc in next dc, patt to last 2 sts, miss 1dc, 1dc in 2nd ch.

Next row Using C, 1sc in first dc, 2ch, 1dc in next dc, patt to last st, 1dc in 2nd ch. *(33 sts.)*

First inc row Using A, 1sc in first dc, 2ch, 1dc in same place as sc, 1dc in next dc, patt to last st, 2dc in 2nd ch. *(35 sts.)*

2nd inc row Using B, 1sc in first dc, 2ch, 2dc in next dc, 1dc in next dc, patt to last 2 sts, 2dc in next dc, 1dc in 2nd ch. *(37 sts.)*

3rd inc row Using A, 1sc in first dc, 2ch, 2dc in next dc, 1dc in each of foll 2 dc, patt to last 3 sts, 1dc in next dc, 2dc in foll dc, 1dc in 2nd ch. *(39 sts.)*

4th inc row Using C, 1sc in first dc, 2ch, 2dc in next dc, 1dc in each of foll 3 dc, patt to last 4 sts, 1dc in each of next 2dc, 2dc in foll dc, 1dc in 2nd ch. *(41 sts.)* Change to A.

First finishing row 1sc in first dc, 2ch, [2dc in next dc, 1dc in each of foll 2dc, miss 1dc, 1tr in next dc, miss 1dc, 1dc in each of next 2dc, 2dc in foll dc, 1dc in next st] to end.

2nd finishing row 1ch, [1sc in each st] to end. Fasten off.

EDGING

Matching sts, join shoulders.

Row 1 (RS) Join A at lower edge of right front, work 52sc in row ends up right front edge, 2sc in corner, 1sc in each of 6dc along right front neck, 1hdc in next dc, 1dc in each of foll 2dc, 1hdc and 1sc in first row end up right front neck, 2sc in each of next 3 row ends, 1hdc and 1dc in last row end, 1sc in each of first 2 free dc of back neck, * 1hdc in next dc, miss 1dc, 1dc in next dc, miss 1dc, 1hdc in foll dc *, 1sc in each of next 5dc, rep from * to *, 1sc in each of next 2 dc, 1dc and 1hdc in first row end of left front neck, 2sc in each of next 3 row ends, 1sc and 1hdc in last row end,

1dc in each of first 2dc along left front neck, 1hdc in next dc, 1sc in each of next 6dc, 2sc in corner, 52sc in row ends down left front edge. *(161 sts.)*

Row 2 1ch, 1sc in each sc up left front to corner, 2sc in each of 2sc at corner, 1sc in each st around neck, 2sc in each of 2sc at corner, 1sc in each sc down right front. *(165 sts.)*

Buttonhole row 1ch, 1sc in each of first 19sc, 2ch, miss 2sc, [1sc in each of next 6sc, 2ch, miss 2sc] 4 times, 2sc in each of next 2sc, 1sc in each sc around neck, 2sc in each of 2sc at corner, [1sc in each sc] to end.

Row 4 1ch, [1sc in each sc] to corner, 2sc in each of 2sc at corner, [1sc in each sc] around neck, 2sc in each of 2sc at corner, [1sc in each sc and 2sc in each 2ch sp] to end.

Row 5 1ch, [1sc in each sc] to end. Fasten off. Weave in all ends.

TO FINISH

Press according to ball bands. Join sleeve seams and set in sleeves. Sew on buttons.

Pretty Pull-on Hat

This pretty hat couldn't be easier to make. It's all in double crochet, so it grows quickly and it's worked in rounds from the top down, so there's no sewing required except for the decorative flowers. These are made from strips of double crochet gathered and sewn on afterward.

ESTIMATED TIME TO COMPLETE

For the 2nd size hat, 4 hours.

YARN

Debbie Bliss Cashmerino DK (55% merino wool, 33% acrylic) light worsted (DK) weight yarn, approx. 120yd (110m) per 1¾oz (50g) ball 1(**2**:2) balls in Lilac 21

HOOK AND EQUIPMENT

E/4 (3.50mm) crochet hook

Yarn needle

SIZE AND FINISHED MEASUREMENTS

To fit: age 6 months(**1 to 3**:4 to 5 years)
Actual measurement: around head
14¾(**17¾**:20½)in [37.5(**45**:52.5)cm]
Figures in parentheses refer to larger sizes.
One figure refers to all sizes.

GAUGE

16 sts and 10 rows to 4in (10cm) over single crochet worked in rounds using E/4 (3.50mm) hook. Change hook size if necessary to obtain this gauge.

ABBREVIATIONS

ch = chain; **cont** = continue; **dc** = double crochet; **ss** = slip stitch; **st(s)** = stitch(es); [ ] = work instructions in brackets as directed.

TIPS

▨ The hat is worked from the top down, which makes it easy to check the fit as you go.

▨ Work the 3rd chain at the start of each round loosely. This will make it easier to slip the hook under both loops when joining at the end of the round.

▨ Crab stitch is just single crochet worked backward. When edging the ruffles for the flowers, work the crab stitch quite loosely so the edge spreads, making the flowers more ruffled.

▨ If you want to make the hat without the flowers, you'll need just 1(**1**:2) 1¾oz (50g) balls of Cashmerino DK.

HAT

Wind yarn around finger to make a ring.
Round 1 (RS) 3ch, 11dc in ring, pull end to tighten ring, ss in 3rd ch. *(12 sts.)*
Round 2 3ch, 1dc in same place as ss, [2dc in next dc] 11 times, ss in 3rd ch. *(24 sts.)*
Round 3 3ch, 1dc in same place as ss, 1dc in next dc, [2dc in foll dc, 1dc in next dc] 11 times, ss in 3rd ch. *(36 sts.)*
Round 4 3ch, 1dc in same place as ss, 1dc in each of next 2 dc, [2dc in foll dc, 1dc in each of next 2dc] 11 times, ss in 3rd ch. *(48 sts.)*

Cont in this way working one more dc between increases each time, work 1(**2**:3) more increase rounds. *(60(**72**:84) sts.)*
Work 8(**10**:12) rounds straight.
Edging Work 1 round crab stitch. Fasten off.

ROSES

(Make 2)
First ruffle Make 40ch.
Row 1 1dc in 4th ch from hook, [1dc in each ch] to end. *(38 sts.)*
Work 1 row crab st. Fasten off.
2nd ruffle Make 23ch.
Row 1 As Row 1 of first ruffle. *(21 sts.)*

Row 2 3ch, 2dc in first dc, [3dc in each dc] to end, 3dc in top ch. *(63 sts.)*
Work 1 row crab st. Fasten off. Weave in ends (see page 119).

TO FINISH

Gather smooth edge of first ruffle, roll and secure to make flower center. Gather 2nd ruffle, curl around flower center, and secure. Weave in all ends. Sew roses on hat level with ears.

Heirloom Bonnet

The simplest of stitches in sumptuous silk-mix yarn combined with pretty ribbon give an antique heirloom effect to this traditional bonnet. The shape is very simple, too, so it's easy and quick to make.

ESTIMATED TIME TO COMPLETE

The bonnet took 2½ hours

ABOUT THIS YARN

Sirdar Snuggly Cashmere Merino Silk DK (75% merino wool, 20% silk, 5% cashmere) light worsted (DK) weight yarn, approx. 127yd (116m) per 1¾oz (50g) ball
   1 ball in Mother Goose 301 (cream)
24in (60cm) length of narrow ribbon

SIZE AND FINISHED MEASUREMENT

To fit: age newborn to 6 months
Actual measurement: around brim
13½in (34cm)

HOOKS AND EQUIPMENT

E/4 (3.50mm) and F/5 (4.00mm) crochet hooks
Yarn needle

GAUGE

15 sts and 13 rows to 4in (10cm) over double crochet-groups patt using F/5 (4.00mm) hook. Change hook size if necessary to obtain this gauge.

ABBREVIATIONS

ch = chain; **cont** = continue; **dc** = double crochet; **3dctog** = leaving last loop of each st on hook, work 3dc, yoh and pull though 4 loops on hook; **dec** = decrease; **rep** = repeat; **RS** = right side; **sc** = single crochet; **2sctog** = insert hook in first st, yoh and pull through, insert hook in 2nd st, yoh and pull through, yoh and pull through 3 loops on hook; **sp** = space; **ss** = slip stitch; **st(s)** = stitch(es); **WS** = wrong side; **yoh** = yarn over hook; **[ ]** = work instructions in brackets as directed.

TIPS

▪ If you want longer ties, make more chain at each side of the lower edging.

▪ You can fold back the shell edging if desired, to make a pretty brim to frame the baby's face.

BONNET

Using F/5 (4.00mm) hook, make 5ch, ss in first ch to form a ring. Pull yarn to tighten ring.
Row 1 1ch, 7sc in ring, turn.
Row 2 (RS) 1sc in first sc, 2ch, 2dc in same place as sc, [3dc in each sc] to end. *(21 sts.)*
Row 3 1ch, 1sc in first dc, [2ch, miss 1dc, 1sc in next dc] 9 times, 2ch, miss 1dc, 1sc in 2nd ch.

Row 4 1sc in first sc, 2ch, 3dc in each 2ch sp, 1dc in last sc. *(32 sts.)*
Row 5 3ch, [miss 1dc, 1sc in next dc, 2ch] 15 times, 1sc in 2nd ch.
Row 6 As Row 4, working last dc in first ch.
Row 7 As Row 5, repeating instructions in brackets 24 times.
Row 8 As Row 6. *(77 sts.)*
Row 9 1sc in first dc, 2ch, miss first 4dc, [2dc between each 3dc group] to last 4 sts, miss 3dc, 1dc in 2nd ch. *(50 sts.)*

Row 10 1sc in first dc, 2ch, 2dc between first dc and first 2dc group, [2dc between each 2dc group] to end, 2dc after last 2dc group, 1dc in 2nd ch. *(52 sts.)*
Row 11 1sc in first dc, 2ch, miss first 3dc, [2dc between each 2dc group] to end, miss 2dc, 1dc in 2nd ch. *(50 sts.)*
Work Rows 10 and 11 rows 3 more times.
Row 18 1ch, [1sc in each dc] to end, 1sc in ch.

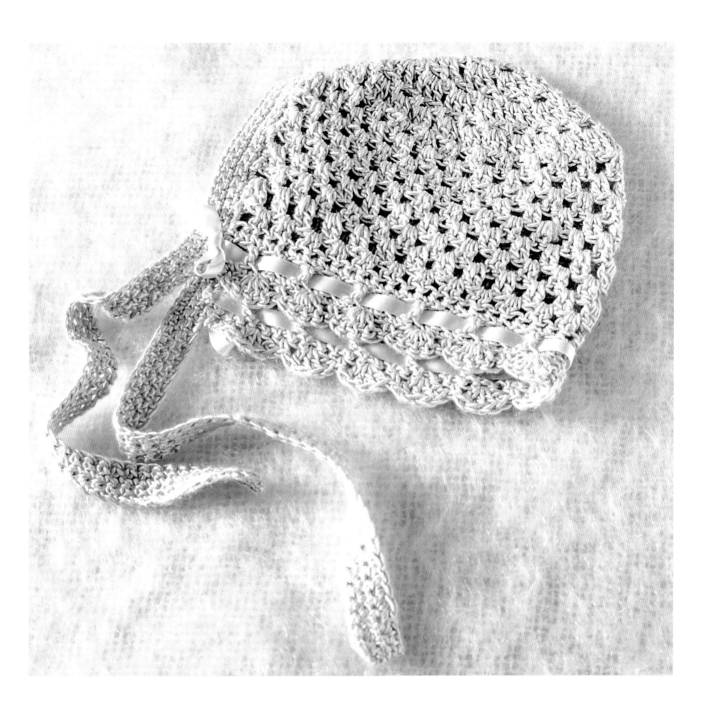

Row 19 4ch, [miss 1sc, 1dc in next sc, 1ch] to end, omitting last ch.

Row 20 1ch, 1sc in first dc, [1sc in next sp, 1sc in next dc] to end, working last sc in 3rd ch. *(51 sts.)*

Row 21 1ch, 1sc in each of first 2sc, [miss 1sc, 4dc in next sc, miss 1sc, 1sc in foll sc] 12 times, 1sc in last sc. Fasten off. Weave in ends (see page 119).

TIES

Join first 8 rows to form back seam. Using F/5 (4.00mm) hook, make 40ch, change to E/4 (3.50mm) hook and with RS facing, work 44sc along lower edge of bonnet, change to F/5 (4.00mm) hook, make 41ch. Change to E/4 (3.50mm) hook.

Row 1 1sc in 2nd ch from hook, 1sc in each of next 39ch, 1sc in each of 44sc, 1sc in each of last 40ch. *(124 sts.)*

Work 3 rows sc. Fasten off. Weave in ends.

TO FINISH

Press according to ball band. Making tiny bows at each side, thread ribbon through eyelet band, stitching at each end to secure the bows.

Heirloom Bootees

These charming little bootees are worked in the round from the toes upward, in single crochet with a shell edging to match the Heirloom Bonnet on pages 80–81.

ESTIMATED TIME TO COMPLETE

It took 4 hours for the pair.

ABOUT THIS YARN

Sirdar Snuggly Cashmere Merino Silk DK (75% merino wool, 20% silk, 5% cashmere) light worsted (DK) weight yarn, approx. 127yd (116m) per 1¾oz (50g) ball
1 ball in Mother Goose 301 (cream)
24in (61cm) length of narrow ribbon

HOOK AND EQUIPMENT

E/4 (3.50mm) crochet hook

Yarn needle

SIZE AND FINISHED MEASUREMENT

To fit: newborn to 6 months
Actual measurements: along sole 3½in (9cm)

GAUGE

21 sts and 24 rows to 4in (10cm) over single crochet using E/4 (3.50mm) hook. Change hook size if necessary to obtain this gauge.

ABBREVIATIONS

See Heirloom Bonnet on page 80.

TIPS

■ If you'd like to make the bootees longer or shorter in the foot and at the ankle, simply work an even number of rows until you reach the length you require.

BOOTEES

Left bootee Make 8ch.

Round 1 2sc in 2nd ch from hook, 1sc in each of next 5ch, 4sc in last ch, cont working into base of ch, 1sc in each of next 5ch, 2sc in last ch, ss in first sc. *(18 sts.)*

Round 2 1ch, 2sc in first sc, 1sc in each of next 7sc, 2sc in each of foll 2sc, 1sc in each of next 7sc, 2sc in last sc, ss in first sc. *(22 sts.)*

Round 3 1ch, 2sc in first sc, 1sc in each of next 9sc, 2sc in each of foll 2sc, 1sc in each of next 9sc, 2sc in last sc, ss in first sc. *(26 sts.)*

Round 4 1ch, 1sc in same place as ss, [1sc in each sc] to end, ss in first sc, turn.

Cont in sc turning each time, work 15 more rounds **.

Heel opening. Round 1 (RS) Make 13ch loosely, miss 13sc, 1sc in each of next 13sc, ss in first ch, turn.

Round 2 1ch, 1sc in each of 13sc, 1sc in each of next 13ch, ss in first sc, turn. *(26 sts.)*

Cont in sc turning each time, work 3 rounds.

Eyelet round (WS) 1sc in first sc, 3ch, miss 1sc, [1dc in next sc, 1ch, miss 1sc] to end, ss in 2nd ch, turn.

Next round 1ch, 1sc in same place as ss, [1sc in next sp, 1sc in next dc] to last sp, 1sc in last sp, ss in first sc, turn.

Work 1 round sc, turn.

Inc round (RS) 1ch, 1sc in each of first 2sc, * [2sc in next sc, 1sc in each of next 3sc] twice, 2sc in foll sc *,

1sc in each of next 4sc, rep from * to *, 1sc in each of last 2sc, ss in first sc, turn. *(32 sts.)*

Edging round 1ch, [miss 1sc, 4dc in next sc, miss 1sc, 1sc in next sc] to end, ss in first ch. Fasten off.

Heel With RS facing, join yarn in base of first ch at heel opening.

Round 1 (RS) 1ch, 1sc in same place as join, 1sc in base of each of next 12ch, 1sc in each of next 13sc, ss in first sc, turn. *(26 sts.)*

Work 1 round sc, turn.

Round 3 1ch, 2sctog, 1sc in each of next 9sc, [2sctog] twice, 1sc in each of next 9sc, 2sctog, ss in first st, turn. *(22 sts.)*

Round 4 1ch, 2sctog, 1sc in each of next 7sc, [2sctog] twice, 1sc in each of next 7sc, 2sctog, ss in first st. 18 sts. Fasten off.

Right bootee Work as left bootee to **.

Heel opening. Round 1 1ch, 1sc in each of 13sc, make 13ch loosely, ss in first sc, turn.

Round 2 1ch, 1sc in each of next 13ch, 1sc in each of next 13sc, ss in first sc, turn. *(26 sts.)*

Complete as given for left bootee.

TO FINISH

Join 9 sts from each side to close heel seams. Weave in ends (see page 119). Cut ribbon in half, thread through eyelet rounds, and tie at front.

Sugar Plum Fairy Cardigan

This snug-fitting wrap-over top is worked in double crochet with a simple shell edging. It's very quick to make because each row gets you one centimeter nearer to finishing. Choose classic soft pink or match the cardigan to a favorite print dress.

ESTIMATED TIME TO COMPLETE

The first size took 5 hours.

YARN AND MATERIALS

Debbie Bliss Cashmerino DK (55% merino wool, 33% acrylic) light worsted (DK) weight yarn, approx. 120yd (110m) per 1¾oz (50g) ball
   3(**4**:**5**:**5**) balls in Petal 22

2 buttons (optional)

SIZE AND FINISHED MEASUREMENTS

To fit: age 3 to 6 months(**1 to 2**:2 to 3:**3 to 4**) years; **chest** 18(**20**:22:**24**)in [46(**51**:56:**61**)cm]
Actual measurements: chest 20½(**22½**:24½:**26½**)in [52.5(**57.5**:62.5:**67.5**)cm]; **length** 6¾(**7½**:9:**9¾**)in [17(**19**:23:**25**)cm]; **sleeve** 7½(**8¼**:9¾:**10½**)in [19(**21**:25:**27**)cm]. Figures in parentheses refer to larger sizes. One figure refers to all sizes.

HOOK AND EQUIPMENT

E/4 (3.50mm) crochet hook
Yarn needle

GAUGE

16 sts and 10 rows to 4in (10cm) over double crochet using E/4 (3.50mm) hook. Change hook size if necessary to obtain this gauge.

ABBREVIATIONS

beg = beginning; **ch** = chain; **cont** = continue; **dc** = double crochet; **2dctog** = leaving last loop of each st on hook, work 2dc, yarn around hook and pull through 3 loops on hook; **inc** = increase; **RS** = right side; **sc** = single crochet; **ss** = slip stitch; **st(s)** = stitch(es); **WS** = wrong side; **yoh** = yarn over hook; **[ ]** = work instructions in brackets as directed.

NOTE

The wrap is worked from the top down, so the lower edge is soft and flexible.

TIPS

▓ Work the starting chain loosely; if necessary use a larger hook.

▓ Buttons are safer for babies, but ties give a more authentic ballet look on the children's sizes. Choose the fastening you prefer.

▓ Babies and children of the same age can be very different sizes, so check the measurements against a garment that you know fits the child well when choosing which size to make.

▓ If you really can't bear to do a gauge swatch, get started on the back and check the width after 7 rows. If your back measures 7¼(**8¼**:9¼:**10¼**)in [18.5(**21**:23.5:**26**)cm] across, and 5 of the 7 rows measure 2in (5cm), you're fine to continue.

▓ When working the edging, work two surface chain into each row, with one chain extra on each front for the 2nd and 4th sizes.

BACK

Make 32(**36**:40:**44**) ch.
Row 1 (WS) 1dc in 4th ch from hook, [1dc in each ch] to end. (*30(**34**:38:**42**) sts.*)
Row 2 1sc in first dc, 2ch, [1dc in each dc] to last st, 1dc in last ch. Row 2 forms dc.
Cont in dc, work 7(**8**:9:**10**) more rows.
Shape armholes. Inc row. 1sc in first dc, 2ch, 1dc in same dc as sc, [1dc in each dc] to last st, 2dc in 2nd ch.
Cont in dc, inc in this way at each end of next row. (*34(**38**:42:**46**) sts.*) Fasten off.
Next row Make 4ch, 2dc in first dc, [1dc in each dc] to last st, 2dc in 2nd ch, make 6ch. (*36(**40**:44:**48**) dc.*)
Next row 1dc in 4th ch from hook, 1dc in each of next 2ch, [1dc in each dc], 1dc in each of 4ch. (*44(**48**:52:**56**) sts.*)
Cont in dc, work 4(**5**:8:**9**) rows.
Fasten off.

RIGHT FRONT

Make 11(**12**:13:**14**)ch.
Work Row 1 as given for back. (*9(**10**:11:**12**) sts.*)
Cont in dc as back, work 2 rows **.
Shape front. Row 4 (RS) 1sc in first dc, 2ch, [1dc in each dc] to last st, 2dc in 2nd ch.
Row 5 1sc in first dc, 2ch, 1dc in same dc as sc, [1dc in each dc] to last st, 1dc in 2nd ch.
Cont in dc, inc one st at front edge in

same way as Rows 4 and 5 on next 4(**5**:6:**7**) rows. *(15(**17**:19:**21**) sts.)*

Shape armhole Inc in same way as back at each end of next 2(**3**:2:**3**) rows. *(19(**23**:23:**27**) sts.)*

1st and 3rd sizes Fasten off.

Next row (RS) Make 4ch, 2dc in first dc, [1dc in each dc] to last st, 2dc in 2nd ch.

Next row 1sc in first dc, 2ch, 1dc in same dc as sc, [1dc in each dc] to last dc, 1dc in each of next 4ch.

2nd and 4th sizes Do not turn at end of last row, make 6ch.

Next row (RS) 1dc in 4th ch from hook, 1dc in each of next 2ch, [1dc in each dc] to last st, 2dc in 2nd ch.

All sizes *(26(**28**:30:**32**) sts.)* Cont in dc, inc at front edge on next 4(**5**:8:**9**) rows. *(30(**33**:38:**41**) sts.)* Fasten off.

LEFT FRONT

Work as given for right front to **.

Shape front Cont in dc, inc 1 st at beg of next row and at this edge on next 5(**6**:7:**8**) rows. *(15(**17**:19:**21**) sts.)*

Shape armhole Inc in same way as back at each end of next 3(**2**:3:**2**) rows. *(21(**21**:25:**25**) sts.)*

1st and 3rd sizes Do not turn at end of last row, make 6ch.

Next row (WS) 1dc in 4th ch from hook, 1dc in each of next 2ch, [1dc in each dc] to last st, 2dc in 2nd ch.

2nd and 4th sizes Fasten off.

Next row (WS) Make 4ch, 2dc in first dc, [1dc in each dc] to last st, 2dc in 2nd ch.

Next row 1sc in first dc, 2ch, 1dc in same dc as sc, [1dc in each dc] to last dc, 1dc in each of next 4ch.

All sizes 26(**28**:30:**32**) sts. Cont in dc, inc at front edge on next 4(**5**:8:**9**) rows. *(30(**33**:38:**41**) sts.)* Fasten off.

SLEEVES

Make 27(**29**:31:**33**) ch.
Work Row 1 as given for back. *(25(**27**:29:**31**) sts.)*

Cont in dc as for back, work 2(**2**:4:**3**) rows, then inc one st at each end of next row in same way as back and at each end of 4(**5**:6:**7**) foll **3rd rows.** *(35(**39**:43:**47**) sts.)*

Inc at each end of next 3(**2**:1:**1**) rows. *(41(**43**:45:**49**) sts.)*

Shape top. Row 1 Ss in each of first 4dc, 1sc in next dc, 2ch, 1dc in each dc to last 4 sts, turn. *(33(**35**:37:**41**) sts.)*

Dec row 1sc in first dc, 1ch, [1dc in each dc] to last 2 sts, 2dctog. Cont in dc, work dec row 3(**4**:4:**5**) more times. *(25(**25**:27:**29**) sts.)* Fasten off.

EDGING

Matching sts, join shoulders. With RS facing, join yarn at lower edge of right front. Inserting hook close to edge, work 34(**39**:46:**51**) surface chain up right front edge, 12(**14**:16:**22**) across back neck sts and 34(**39**:46:**51**) down left front edge.

Row 1 (WS) 1ch, 1sc into edge and over each surface chain. *(80(**92**:108:**124**) sts.)*

Row 2 [Miss 1sc, 4dc in next sc, miss 1sc, ss in next sc] to end. Fasten off. Weave in ends (see page 119).

TO FINISH

Press according to ball band. Set in sleeves. Taking 1 st in from each side, join side and sleeve seams. Either overlap fronts and sew on buttons, slipping buttons between stitches to fasten, or make ties and sew on ends of fronts.

TIES

Make 4ch, yoh, insert hook in 4th ch from hook, yoh and pull through, [yoh and pull through] twice, inserting hook in 2 strands at top of previous st each time, cont working a dc chain in this way until tie measures 21½(**24**:25½:**28**)in [55(**61**:65:**71**)cm]. Fasten off. Weave in ends.

Baby Mary Janes

All you need to know is chain, single crochet, and slip stitch to make these adorable little shoes. Each one is worked in the round, starting at the center of the sole, so there's no sewing up, apart from attaching the straps, and there are no seams to rub tiny feet.

ESTIMATED TIME TO COMPLETE

The pair took 3 hours.

YARN AND MATERIALS

Debbie Bliss Cashmerino DK (55% merino wool, 33% acrylic) light worsted (DK) weight yarn, approx. 120yd (110m) per 1¾oz (50g) ball
   1 ball in Petal 22

2 small buttons

HOOK AND EQUIPMENT

E/4 (3.50mm) crochet hook

Yarn needle

SIZE AND FINISHED MEASUREMENTS

To fit: age 3 to 6 months
Actual measurement: along sole approximately 3½in (9cm)

GAUGE

6 rounds of single crochet shaped as given for sole measure 3⅛in (9cm) in length and 2⅛in (5.5cm) wide using E/4 (3.50mm) hook. Change hook size if necessary to obtain this size sole.

ABBREVIATIONS

ch = chain; **cont** = continue; **RS** = right side; **sc** = single crochet; **2sctog** = insert hook in first st, yoh and pull through, insert hook in next st, yoh and pull through, yoh and pull through 3 loops on hook; **ss** = slip st; **st(s)** = stitch(es); **yoh** = yarn over hook; **[ ]** = work instructions in brackets as directed.

TIPS

▨ When pressing the shoes, coax one toe to the left and one to the right to make a pair.

▨ The straps will curve, so use the ends to sew one strap in place and a separate length of yarn to sew the smooth end to the other instep; hide the ends when sewing on the buttons.

▨ The buttons are simply for decoration. If you prefer, you could embroider bullion knots or sew on ribbon roses.

SHOES

Sole Wrap yarn around finger to make a ring.

Round 1 (RS) 1ch, 8sc in ring, pull end to tighten ring, ss in first sc, make 6ch.

Round 2 2sc in 2nd ch from hook, 1sc in each of next 4ch, 1sc in each of next 2sc, 2sc in each of foll 4sc, 1sc in each of next 2sc, 1sc in base of next 4ch, 2sc in base of last ch, ss in first sc. *(24 sts.)*

Round 3 1ch, 2sc in first sc, 1sc in each of next 9sc, 2sc in foll sc, 1sc in each of next 2sc, 2sc in foll sc, 1sc in each of next 9sc, 2sc in last sc, ss in first sc. *(28 sts.)*

Round 4 1ch, 2sc in each of first 2sc, 1sc in each of next 9sc, 2sc in each of foll 2sc, 1sc in each of next 2sc, 2sc in each of foll 2 sc, 1sc in each of next 9sc, 2sc in each of last 2sc, ss in first sc. *(36 sts.)*

Round 5 1ch, 1sc in first sc, 2sc in foll sc, 1sc in each of next 13sc, 2sc in foll sc, 1sc in each of next 4sc, 2sc in foll sc, 1sc in each of next 13sc, 2sc in foll sc, 1sc in last sc, ss in first sc. *(40 sts.)*

Round 6 1ch, [1sc in each sc] to end, ss in first sc. Round 6 forms sc.

Upper Work 3 more rounds sc.

Shape front. Round 1 1ch, 1sc in each of first 16sc, [2sctog, 1sc in next sc] twice, 2sctog, 1sc in each of last 16sc, ss in first sc. *(37 sts.)*

Round 2 1ch, 1sc in each of first 14sc, [2sctog] twice, 1sc in next sc, [2sctog] twice, 1sc in each of last 14sc, ss in first sc. 33 sts. Fasten off.

Strap Make 12ch. 1sc in 2nd ch from hook, [1sc in each ch] to end. Fasten off.

Make second shoe and strap.

TO FINISH

Press according to ball band. Sew straps on inner edges of shoes. Sew on buttons to hold ends of straps in place.

Enchanting Blue Elephant

This toy is worked all in very firm single crochet, mostly in the round, so the shape is very sculptural and the construction very strong. Add button eyes and fabric tongue and tusks as shown in the pictures if you're making the elephant for an older child or embroider the features if you're giving the toy to a baby or very young child.

ESTIMATED TIME TO COMPLETE

8 hours

YARN AND MATERIALS

Rico Essentials Cotton DK (100% cotton) light worsted (DK) weight yarn, approx. 131yd (120m) per 1¾oz (50g) ball
   3 balls in Denim 108

Washable polyester fiberfill

Four 1½ x 1¼in (4 x 3cm) ovals of soft leather or felt

2 small domed buttons and strong thread

1 pink and two cream 4 x 4in (10 x 10cm) squares of fabric and matching sewing thread

FINISHED MEASUREMENT

Height (to shoulder) 6½in (16.5cm)

HOOK AND EQUIPMENT

D/3 (3.00mm) crochet hook

Yarn needle

Sharp needle (optional)

GAUGE

16 sts and 20 rows to 4in (10cm) over single crochet worked in turning rounds using D/3 (3.00mm) hook. Change hook size if necessary to obtain this gauge.

ABBREVIATIONS

beg = beginning; **ch** = chain; **cont** = continue; **inc** = increase; **RS** = right side; **sc** = single crochet; **2sctog** = insert hook in first st and pull loop through, insert hook in 2nd st and pull loop through, yarn around hook and pull through 3 loops on hook; **ss** = slip stitch; **st(s)** = stitch(es); **WS** = wrong side; **[ ]** = work instructions in brackets as directed.

NOTES

The hook size and gauge given are tighter than would normally be used with this yarn, to make a firm fabric and a sculptural shape.

If the elephant is for a baby or very small child, embroider the eyes, tongue and tusks with black, pink, and cream yarn.

TIPS

- Don't put too much fiberfill in the trunk. Shape the face with small balls of fiberfill pushed into the cheeks and forehead before you fill the head with larger wads of fiberfill.

- If you want your elephant to stand up, pack the legs firmly to near the top, then pin the legs onto the body to find the best point of balance before stitching; add fiberfill if necessary.

- Go over each seam twice to make sure that the stitching is secure.

- As with all handmade toys, check every now and then for wear and tear and redo any stitching if necessary.

- Much of the elephant is worked in the round; join seams and sew on the legs and ears firmly.

HEAD AND BODY

Trunk Make 10ch, ss in first ch to form a ring.

Round 1 1ch, [working into back loop only, 1sc in each ch] to end, ss in first sc, turn. *(10 sts.)*

Round 2 (RS) 1ch, 1sc in first sc, [2sctog] 4 times, 1sc in last sc, ss in first sc, turn. *(6 sts.)*

Round 3 1ch, [1sc in each st] to end, ss in first sc, turn.

Round 3 forms sc. Turning each time, work 4 more rounds.

Round 8 1ch, 2sc in first sc, [1sc in each sc] to last sc, 2sc in last sc, ss in first sc, turn. *(8 sts.)*

Cont in sc, turning each time, inc in this way at beg and end of next 3 RS rounds. *(14 sts.)*

Next row (WS) 1ch, [1sc in each sc] to end, do not join in a round, turn.

Cont in sc, working in rows and turning after each row.

Face. **Row 1 (RS) 1ch, [2sc in each sc] to end. *(28 sts.)*

Row 2 1ch, [1sc in each sc] to end.

Row 3 1ch, 1sc in each of first 9sc, 2sc in each of next 2sc, 1sc in each of foll 6sc, 2sc in each of next 2sc, 1sc in each of last 9sc. *(32 sts.)* **.

Row 4 1ch, 1sc in each of first 9sc, 2sc in each of next 4sc, 1sc in each of foll 6sc, 2sc in each of next 4sc, 1sc in each of last 9sc. *(40 sts.)*

Cont in sc, work 2 rows.

Shape cheeks. Next row (RS) 1ch, 1sc in first sc, [2sctog] 3 times, 1sc in each of next 26sc, [2sctog] 3 times, 1sc in last sc. *(34 sts.)*

Shape mouth. Next round With RS together, join first 3 and last 3 sts of previous row with sc, 1ch, [1sc in each sc] to end, ss in first sc after 1ch to join in a round, turn. *(28 sts.)*
Turning each time, work 4 rounds sc.

Shape chest and neck. Round 1 (RS) 1ch, 2sc in each of first 3sc, 1sc in each of next 5sc, [2sctog] twice, 1sc in each of next 4sc, [2sctog] twice, 1sc in each of next 5sc, 2sc in each of last 3sc, ss in first sc, turn. *(30 sts.)*

Round 2 1ch, 2sc in each of first 3sc, [1sc in each sc] to last 3sc, 2sc in each of last 3sc, ss in first sc, turn. *(36 sts.)*

Round 3 1ch, [1sc in each of next 2sc, 2sc in foll sc] 3 times, [1sc in each sc] to last 9sc, [2sc in next sc, 1sc in each of foll 2sc] 3 times, ss in first sc, turn. *(42 sts.)*

Make up and stuff head and body
Stitch end of trunk in a V shape and stuff trunk lightly. Join row ends of face. Fold corners of each cream square

together to make a triangle, fold long edges together, then roll and stitch to form cone-shaped tusks. Insert points of tusks from WS through between stitches at each side of mouth; the bulk of the fabric will make it impossible to pull through more than a small amount. Stitch in place and stuff around tusks, shaping face. Fold pink fabric in the same way but making a flatter tongue shape at the point, insert in mouth; and stitch to secure.

Stuff face Mark positions for eyes and ears. Knot shank of button in the center of a doubled length of strong thread. Using a large, sharp needle, thread one end, insert in right eye and bring out at right ear, thread the other end, insert in right eye and bring out at left ear. Do the same with the other button for the left eye, bringing ends out a few stitches apart. Pull ends to make eye sockets, firmly knot the threads together, weave in ends (see page 119) and trim.
Stuff head; stuff body before working the last few rounds of the bottom shaping.

Body Cont in sc and turning each time, work 11 rounds.

Shape tummy. Next round (RS) 1ch, 1sc in first sc, 2sc in each of next 3sc, [1sc in each sc] to last 4sc, 2sc in each of next 3sc, 1sc in last sc, ss in first sc, turn. *(48 sts.)*
Cont in sc turning each time, work 9 rounds.

Shape bottom. Round 1 (RS) 1ch, 1sc in each of first 15sc, [2sctog, 1sc in each of next 2sc] 5 times, 1sc in each of last 13sc, ss in first sc, turn. 43 sts. Work 1 round.

Round 3 1ch, 1sc in each of first 3sc, [2sctog, 1sc in each of next 3sc] 8 times, ss in first sc, turn. *(35 sts.)*

Round 4 1ch, 1sc in each of first 3sc, [2sctog, 1sc in each of next 2sc] 8 times, ss in first sc, turn. *(27 sts.)*

Round 5 1ch, 1sc in each of first 3sc, [2sctog, 1sc in each of next 2sc] 6 times, ss in first sc, turn. *(21 sts.)*

Round 6 1ch, 1sc in first sc, [2sctog] 10 times, ss in first sc. *(11 sts.)*
Finish stuffing body.

Round 7 1ch, 1sc in first st, [2sctog] 5 times, ss in first sc, do not turn. *(6 sts.)*

Tail. Next round 1ch, [2sctog] 3 times, ss in first st. *(3 sts.)*
Cont working in a spiral for 6 more sc, work 2ch, fasten off. Add more strands of yarn through ch at end of tail; stitch and trim to form a small tassel.

LEGS

Front legs Make 18ch, ss in first ch to form a ring.
Turning each time, work 3 rounds sc. Insert oval footpads and stitch firmly to starting ch.

Shape foot. Next round (RS) 1ch, 1sc in each of first 5sc, [2sctog, 1sc in next sc] 3 times, 1sc in each of last 4sc, ss in first sc, turn. 15 sts ***.
Cont in sc and turning each time, work 13 rounds. Fasten off. Weave in ends.

Back legs Work as given for front legs to ***. Cont in sc turning each time, work 11 rounds. Fasten off.

EARS

Make 15ch.

Row 1 1sc in 2nd ch from hook, [1sc in each ch] to end. *(14 sts.)*
Work as given for face from ** to **. Work 1 more row sc. Fasten off.

TO FINISH

Stuff legs and sew in place on body. Sew on ears. Weave in ends.

Friendly Zebra

The zebra is worked in firm single crochet, mostly in the round. Using buttons for the eyes is optional; if you're making the toy for a baby, embroider the eyes instead. It's a really nice touch to make the zebra stand up on flexible legs reinforced with plastic-coated wire but if you're making the toy for a baby, leave the wire out and stuff the legs firmly.

ESTIMATED TIME TO COMPLETE

The zebra took 7 hours.

YARN AND MATERIALS

Rico Essentials Cotton DK (100% cotton) light worsted (DK) weight yarn, approx. 131yd (120m) per 1¾oz (50g) ball
1 ball in each of
Black 90 (A)
Cream 88 (B)

Washable polyester fiberfill

Pink embroidery floss

2 small buttons and strong thread (optional)

4 x 9½in (24cm) lengths of plastic-coated wire (optional)

HOOK AND EQUIPMENT

D/3 (3.00mm) crochet hook

Yarn needle

Sharp needle (optional)

FINISHED MEASUREMENT

Height (to shoulder) 7½in (19cm)

GAUGE

16 sts and 20 rows to 4in (10cm) over double-crochet stripe patt worked in turning rounds using D/3 (3.00mm) hook. Change hook size if necessary to obtain this gauge.

ABBREVIATIONS

ch = chain; **cont** = continue; **patt** = pattern; **RS** = right side; **sc** = single crochet; **2sctog** = insert hook in first st and pull loop through, insert hook in 2nd st and pull loop through, yarn over hook and pull through 3 loops on hook; **ss** = slip stitch; **st(s)** = stitch(es); **WS** = wrong side; **[ ]** = work instructions in brackets as directed.

NOTES

The hook size and gauge given are tighter than would usually be used with this yarn to make a firm fabric and a sculptural shape.

The construction is strong but make sure that you join seams and sew on the legs, ears, tail, and mane firmly.

If you are making the zebra for a baby or very small child, embroider the eyes.

TIPS

▨ Leave a long end when making the ring at the start of the head. Pinch the first few rounds together and use the end to stitch the rounds into a triangular mouth shape. Do this while you can still get your fingers inside!

▨ As with all handmade toys, check every now and then for wear and tear, and redo any stitching if necessary.

HEAD AND BODY

Shape nose Using A, wind yarn around finger to form a ring. Pull end to tighten ring.

Round 1 (RS) 1ch, 9sc in ring, ss in first sc, turn. *(9 sts.)*

Round 2 1ch, [1sc in each sc] to end, ss in first sc, turn.

Round 3 1ch, 2sc in first sc, [1sc in each of next 2sc, 3sc in next sc] twice, 1sc in each of next 2sc, 1sc in same sc as first 2sc, ss in first sc, turn. *(15 sts.)*

Round 4 1ch, [1sc in each sc] to end, ss in first sc, turn.
Round 4 forms sc.

Round 5 1ch, 1sc in each of first 5sc, [4sc in next sc, 1sc in each of next 4sc] twice, ss in first sc, turn. *(21 sts.)*
Work 1 round sc, turn.

Change to B. Work 2 rounds sc, turning at the end of each round.

Change to A. Work 2 rounds sc, turning at the end of each round.
The last 4 rows form the stripe patt.
Cont in sc stripe patt, work 3 rows.

Shape head. Round 1 (WS) 1ch, 1sc in each of first 8sc, 2sc in each of next 6sc, 1sc in each of last 7sc, ss in first sc, turn. *(27 sts.)*
Work 1 round.

Round 3 1ch, 1sc in each of first 12sc, 2sc in each of next 4sc, 1sc in each of last 11sc, ss in first sc, turn. (31 sts.)
Work 1 round sc. Fasten off.
With WS facing, join A in 4th sc to left of join in previous row.

** Neck. Row 1 1ch, 1sc in same place as join, 1sc in each of next 23sc, turn. Cont changing colors for stripe patt.

Row 2 1ch, miss first sc, 1sc in each of next 22sc, turn.

Row 3 1ch, miss first sc, 1sc in each of next 20sc, turn.

Row 4 1ch, miss first sc, 1sc in each of next 18sc, turn.

Row 5 1ch, miss first sc, 1sc in each of next 16sc, turn.

Row 6 1ch, miss first sc, 1sc in each of next 14sc, turn.

Row 7 1ch, miss first sc, 1sc in each of next 12sc, turn.

Row 8 1ch, miss first sc, 1sc in each of next 10sc, turn.

Row 9 1ch, miss first sc, 1sc in each of next 8sc, turn.

Row 10 1ch, miss first sc, 1sc in each of next 6sc, turn.

Rows 11 and 12 1ch, 1sc in each sc. *(6 sts.)*

Row 13 1ch, 2sc in first sc, 1sc in next sc, 2sc in each of next 2sc, 1sc in foll sc, 2sc in last sc. 10 sts. Work 1 row.

Row 15 1ch, 2sc in first sc, 1sc in each of next 3sc, 2sc in each of foll 2sc, 1sc in each of next 3sc, 2sc in last sc. *(14 sts.)*
Work 1 row.

Row 17 1ch, 2sc in first sc, 1sc in each of next 5sc, 2sc in each of foll 2sc, 1sc in each of next 5sc, 2sc in last sc. *(18 sts.)*
Work 1 row.

Row 19 1ch, 2sc in first sc, 1sc in each of next 7sc, 2sc in each of foll 2sc, 1sc in each of next 7sc, 2sc in last sc. *(22 sts.)*
Work 1 row. Fasten off.
With WS facing, join A in center st at front neck.

Joining round (WS) 1ch, 1sc in same place as join, 1sc in each of next 3sc across front neck, 1sc in corner, 1sc in each of 22sc around back neck, 1sc in front neck corner, 1sc in each of

last 3sc across front neck, ss in first sc, turn. *(31 sts)* **.
Cont in stripe patt, work 2 more rounds sc.

Next round (RS) 1ch, 1sc in each of next 14sc, 2sc in next sc, 1sc in each of next 14sc, 2sctog, ss in first sc. *(31 sts.)* Fasten off.

Shape chest Count back 12 sts from join and join A in this 12th st. Work as given for neck from ** to **, joining in at center back neck before working Joining round and reading back for front on Joining round. Using pink thread, embroider tongue; using B, embroider teeth. Fasten off.

Body Join yarn at opposite side of round so joins will be under tummy. Cont in sc stripe patt, work 19 more rounds.

Shape bottom. Round 1 (WS) 1ch, 1sc in first sc, [2sctog] twice, [1sc in each sc] to last 4sc, [2sctog] twice, ss in first sc. *(27 sts.)*
Work 1 round.

Round 3 1ch, 1sc in first sc, [2sctog, 1sc in next st] 8 times, 2sctog, ss in first sc, turn. *(18 sts.)*
Work 1 round.

Round 5 1ch, [2sctog] 9 times, ss in first st. 9 sts. Leaving a long end, fasten off.

LEGS

Using A, wrap yarn around finger to form a ring. Pull end to tighten ring.

Round 1 (RS) 1ch, 8sc in ring, ss in first sc, turn. *(8 sts.)*

Round 2 1ch, 2sc in each of first 4sc, 1sc in each of last 4sc, ss in first sc, turn. *(12 sts.)*

Round 3 1ch, 1sc in each sc, ss in first sc, turn.

Round 4 1ch, [2sctog] 4 times, 1sc in each of next 4sc, ss in first sc, turn. *(8 sts.)*
Change to B. Cont in sc stripe patt, work 15 rounds.

Next round (WS) 1ch, 2sc in first sc, [1sc in next sc, 2sc in foll sc] 3 times, 1sc in last sc, ss in first sc, turn. *(12 sts.)*
Cont in sc stripe patt, work 4 rounds. Fasten off. Weave in ends (see page 119).

EARS

Using A, make 5ch.

Row 1 1sc in 2nd ch from hook, [1sc in each ch] to end. *(4 sts.)*
Cont in sc, work 6 rows.

Next row 1ch, [2sctog] twice. *(2 sts.)*

Next row 1ch, 2sctog. Fasten off.

TO FINISH

Using a blunt-pointed needle, thread end through sts of last round of body. Draw up and secure. Press first 3 to 4 rounds at nose inward at an angle, pinch sides together, and stitch with A to form a mouth shape as shown in the picture. Join neck seams and one chest seam.

Stuff head and body. Join remaining chest seam. Using strong thread doubled, stitch one eye in place bringing thread out at opposite ear position. Secure ends. Repeat for second eye. Sew ears on, hiding eye thread ends. Stuff legs, inserting plastic-coated wire if desired—fold in half and wrap in fiberfill with ends turned over to avoid sharp wires protruding. Sew legs on body.

Mane Using A, make 11 tassels each 1¼in (3cm) long. Work a row of surface chain down back neck, sew tassels on chain and trim.

Tail Using A, make a tassel approximately 3½in (9cm) long. Sew in place and trim.

Candy Striped Jacket

Easy-to-work single crochet creates a waffle-like surface that looks very effective in a simple stripe pattern. The construction is simple too; each half of the jacket is worked from the cuff to the center, so when you've worked the first half, your fingers will "know" what to do for the second. The stripes will also help keep track when counting rows.

ESTIMATED TIME TO COMPLETE

The 2nd size jacket took 13 hours.

ABOUT THIS YARN

Debbie Bliss Baby Cashmerino (55% merino wool, 33% acrylic, 12% cashmere) sport (baby) weight yarn, approx. 137yd (125m) per 1¾oz (50g) ball

    3(**3**:4) balls in Ecru 101 (A)

    1(**2**:3) balls in Kingfisher 72 (B)

4 buttons

HOOK AND EQUIPMENT

D/3 (3.00mm) crochet hook

Blunt-pointed needle

SIZE AND FINISHED MEASUREMENTS

To fit: age 3(**6**:12) months;

chest 16(**18**:20)in [41(**46**:51)cm];

height 25(**28¼**:31½)in [64(**72**:80)cm]

Actual measurements:

chest 18(**23½**:28¾)in [46(**60**:73)cm];

length 8½(**10¼**:12¼)in [22(**26**:31.5)cm];

sleeve (with cuff turned back) 5½(**6½**:8½)in [14(**16.5**:21.5)cm]

Figures in parentheses refer to larger sizes. One figure refers to all sizes.

GAUGE

19 sts and 24 rows to 4in (10cm) over single crochet using D/3 (3.00mm) hook. Change hook size if necessary to obtain this gauge.

ABBREVIATIONS

ch = chain; **cont** = continue; **dec** = decrease; **foll** = following; **inc** = increase; **patt** = pattern; **RS** = right side; **sc** = single crochet; **2sctog** = insert hook in next st and pull loop through, insert hook in foll st and pull loop through, yoh and pull through 3 loops on hook; **ss** = slip stitch; **st(s)** = stitch(es); **WS** = wrong side; **yoh** = yarn over hook; **[ ]** = work instructions in brackets as directed.

NOTE

The jacket is worked in two halves and joined at the center back.

TIPS

- It really helps to put markers at each end of the increase rows for the sleeve so you can see at a glance how many increases you have done.

- Make sure you work the chain for the side seam loosely or it will pull up. If necessary, use a hook one or two sizes larger.

- It's okay to carry the A yarn up over the two row ends of the stripe in B, but the B yarn shows up against the four rows in A, so the edge looks better if you cut the B yarn and weave in the ends.

- The back seam will be flatter if you sew the pieces together. You could join the seam with crochet, but it will make a ridge.

- If you want to make the jacket in one color, you'll need approximately 4(**5**:6) x 1¾oz (50g) balls of Debbie Bliss Baby Cashmerino.

- Instructions are given for working buttonholes for a girl in the right front and for a boy in the left front. Omit whichever set of buttonholes is not needed.

RIGHT HALF

Cuff Using A, make 33(**37**:43)ch.

Row 1 1sc in 2nd ch from hook, 1sc in each ch to end. *(32(**36**:42) sts.)*

Row 2 1ch, 1sc in each sc to end.

Row 2 forms single crochet.

Cont in A, work 7(**9**:9) more rows.

Sleeve Cont in sc, work 2 rows B, 4 rows A.

These 6 rows form the stripe patt.

Cont in sc stripe patt, work 2 more rows, ending with a 2nd row in B.

Inc row (RS) Using A, 1ch, 2sc in first sc, [1sc in each sc] to last sc, 2sc in last sc.

Cont in sc stripe patt, inc in this way at each end of 6(**7**:6) foll 4th rows.

3rd size only Inc at each end of 2 foll 6th rows.

All sizes *(46(52:60) sts.)*
Patt 1(3:7) rows, ending with a 2nd row in A, do not turn at end of last row, make 20(25:31)ch loosely.

Back and front. Next row 1sc in 2nd ch from hook, 1sc in each of next 18(23:29)ch, 1sc in each of 46(52:60) sc across sleeve, 1sc in base of 19(24:30)ch. *(84(100:120) sts.)*
Cont in sc stripe patt, work 17(23:29) rows, ending with a 2nd row in A **.

Front neck. Row 1 (RS) 1ch, 1sc in each of 36(44:53)sc, turn and leave 48(56:67)sc.

Row 2 2sctog, 1sc in each sc to end.

Row 3 1ch, 1sc in each sc to last 2 sc, 2sctog. Cont in patt, dec in same way as Rows 2 and 3 on next 1(3:4) rows. *(33(39:47) sts.)*

Boy's jacket Patt 8(8:9) rows.
Fasten off.

Girl's jacket Patt 5(5:6) rows.

Buttonhole row (WS) 1ch, 1sc in first sc, [2ch, miss 2sc, 1sc in each of next 6(7:9)sc] 3 times, 2ch, miss 2sc, 1sc in each of last 6(9:11)sc.

Next row 1ch, 1sc in each sc to 2ch sp, [2sc in 2ch sp, 1sc in each of next 6(7:9)sc] 3 times, 2sc in 2ch sp, 1sc in last sc.
Patt 1 row. Fasten off.

Back neck With RS facing, join A in 8th(8th:9th)sc from first row of front neck.

Row 1 1ch, 1sc in same place as join, 1sc in each sc to end. *(41(49:59) sts.)*
Patt 9(11:13) more rows. Fasten off.

LEFT HALF

Work as given for right half to **.

Back neck. Row 1 (RS) 1ch, 1sc in each of next 41(49:59)sc, turn and leave 43(51:61)sc. Patt 9(11:13) more rows.
Fasten off.

Front neck With RS facing, join yarn in 8th(8th:9th)sc from Row 1 of back neck.

Row 1 1ch, 1sc in each sc to end. *(36(44:53) sc.)*
Cont in patt, dec at neck edge in same way as right front neck on next 3(5:6) rows. *(33(39:47) sts.)*

Girl's jacket Patt 8(8:9) rows.
Fasten off.

Boy's jacket Patt 5(5:6) rows.

Buttonhole row (WS) 1ch, 1sc in each of next 6(9:11)sc, [2ch, miss 2sc, 1sc in each of next 6(7:9)sc] 3 times, 2ch, miss 2sc, 1sc in last sc.

Next row 1ch, 1sc in first sc, [2sc in 2ch sp, 1sc in each of next 6(7:9)sc] 3 times, 2sc in 2ch sp, 1sc in each of last 6(9:11)sc.
Patt 1 row. Fasten off. Weave in ends (see page 119).

COLLAR

Join back seam. With RS facing, join A in 5th row end from right front edge.

Row 1 1ch, 8(10:12)sc in row ends and 1sc in each of 7(7:8)sc up right front neck, 20(24:28)sc across back neck, 1sc in each of 7(7:8)sc and

8(10:12)sc in row ends down left front neck, ending in 5th row end from left front edge. *(50(58:68) sts.)* Work 1 row sc.

Inc row 1ch, 1sc in first sc, * [2sc in next sc, 1sc in each of foll 2sc] 4 times, 2sc in next sc *, 1sc in each of foll 22(30:40)sc, rep from * to *, 1sc in last sc. *(60(68:78) sc.)*
Work 8(8:10) rows sc. Fasten off.

EDGING

With RS facing, join B at center back.

Round 1 Work surface chain as close to the edge as possible in row ends and sts around all edges, turning the chain to the other side for the collar, ss in first ch.

Round 2 1ch, [1sc over each ch] to end, ss in first sc. Fasten off.

TO FINISH

Weave in ends. Press according to ball band. Join sleeve seams. Fold cuff back and work edging in B. Sew on buttons.

Baby Blanket

Sturdy enough to use as a play mat or a stroller cover but soft enough to cuddle up with in a crib, the simple, solid squares that make up this practical little blanket are worked mostly in double crochets, with trebles at the corners, then finished with a border in single crochet. And you'll enjoy the trick that makes working with color in the round neat and easy to do.

ESTIMATED TIME TO COMPLETE

Each square, 40 minutes; blanket, 17 hours.

YARN

Debbie Bliss Cotton DK (100% cotton) light worsted (DK) weight yarn, approx. 92yd (84m) per 1¾oz (50g) ball

    4 balls in Ecru 2 (A)
    4 balls in Duck Egg 9 (B)
    3 balls in Putty 19 (C)

HOOK AND EQUIPMENT

F/5 (4.00mm) crochet hook

Yarn needle

FINISHED MEASUREMENTS

Width 24in (61cm); **length** 29½in (75cm)

GAUGE

Each 5-round square measures 5¼ x 5¼in (13 x 13cm) using F/5 (4.00mm) hook. Change hook size if necessary to obtain this size square.

ABBREVIATIONS

dc = double crochet; **foll** = following; **RS** = right side; **sc** = single crochet; **ss** = slip stitch; **st(s)** = stitch(es); **tr** = treble; **[ ]** = work instructions in brackets as directed.

NOTES

Use the yarn from the center of the ball and the yarn from the outside for opposite color sections or use a separate ball for each section.

When changing colors, always pull through the last loop of the last stitch of the previous section with the new color.

When changing colors on Rounds 4 and 5, say from B to C, work to the last pull-through of the last stitch in B, bring the C yarn back to the start of the section, laying it loosely along the top of the stitches and (except for the first color change of the round) allowing enough extra for the height of the first stitch. Pull through the last stitch in B with C, then catch the strand at the back in with the first stitch and work over the strand as you work into the stitches for that section.

TIPS

▦ Make the last of the chain at the beginning of a round loosely; this will make it easier to work into it when joining the round.

▦ For a neater finish to the squares, don't fasten off in the usual way; instead, pull up the chain from the last stitch until it's about 3in (8cm) long, cut the chain in the center, remove the yarn from the ball, tighten the end, and weave it in.

▦ When working the joining single crochet, hold the squares with wrong sides together, square from below in front and square from above behind, with the top edge slightly protruding; insert hook from RS into square in front and WS into square behind.

▦ Take care not to turn the squares over when you are working the horizontal joins.

PATCHWORK SQUARE

Using A, wind yarn around finger to make a ring.

Round 1 3ch, 11 dc in ring, pull end to close ring, ss in 3rd ch. *(12 sts.)*

Round 2 4ch, 2dc in same place a ss, * 1dc in next dc, [2dc, 1tr] in foll dc, [1tr, 2dc] in next dc, rep from * two more times, 1dc in next dc, [2dc, 1tr] in foll dc, change to B to pull through last loop of last st and ss in 4th ch.

Round 3 Using B work 4ch, 2dc in same place as ss, 1dc in each of next 5dc, [2dc, 1tr] in next tr, using C work * [1tr, 2dc] in foll tr, 1dc in each of next 5dc, [2dc, 1tr] in last tr *, using B, rep from * to *, using C, rep from * to *, pull through last st and ss in 4th ch with B.

Round 4 Using B work 4ch, 1dc in same place as ss, 1dc in each of next 9dc, [1dc, 1tr] in next tr, using C work * [1tr, 1dc] in foll tr, 1dc in each of next 9dc, [1dc, 1tr] in last tr *, using B, rep from * to *, using C, rep from * to *, pull through last st and ss in 4th ch with B.

Round 5 Using B work 4ch, 2dc in same place as ss, 1dc in each of next 11dc, [2dc, 1tr] in next tr, using C work * [1tr, 2dc] in foll tr, 1dc in each of next 11dc, [2dc, 1tr] in last tr *, using B, rep from * to *, using C, rep from * to *. Fasten off.
Make 20 squares.

JOIN SQUARES

Lay squares down in a rectangle that is 4 squares wide by 5 squares long with sections in B at each side and sections in C at top and bottom.
Work the horizontal joins first.

1st line Join A with a sc in first st in C at lower right corner of top right square, * 1sc in st in C at top right corner of square below, [1sc in next st of first square, 1sc in next st of 2nd square] 16 times, 3ch, 1sc in corner of next square above, rep from * to join remaining pairs of squares, ending with 1sc in corner stitch of last square.
Join 2nd line to 3rd, 3rd line to 4th and 4th line to 5th in the same way.
Work vertical joins in the same way, working 1ch, 1sc over 3ch, 1ch between corners of each pair of squares.

BORDER

With RS facing, join A in first st in B at lower right corner.

Round 1 1ch, 2sc in same st as join, * 1sc in each of next 16 sts, [2sc in join, 1sc in each of ncxt 17 sts] 3 times, 2sc in join, 1sc in each of next 16 sts, 2sc in last st of this side, 2sc in first st of next side; work instructions in square brackets twice along top, 3 times down left side and twice along lower edge, rep from * to end, omitting last 2sc, ss in first sc. *(342 sts.)*

Round 2 1ch, 2sc in first sc, * [1sc in each sc] to last st before corner, 2sc in each of next 2sc, rep from * to end, omitting last 2sc, ss in first sc. *(350 sts.)*

Cont in sc increasing at corners in this way on every round, work 1 more round A and 3 rounds B. Fasten off. Weave in ends (see page 119).

Indigo Dye Duffel

This duffel coat is worked all in half double crochet with single crochet seams and crab stitch edging. The nice thing about half double crochet is that it grows fast but is less open than a double crochet fabric, making it ideal for this roomy little duffel coat.

ESTIMATED TIME TO COMPLETE

For the 2nd size duffel, 24 hours.

YARN AND MATERIALS

Rico Essentials Cotton DK (100% cotton) light worsted (DK) weight yarn, approx. 131yd (120m) per 1¾oz (50g) ball
   8(**10**:12) balls in Ocean Blue 112

4 ring and toggle fastenings

48in (122cm) of ⅛in (3mm) wide suede

HOOK AND EQUIPMENT

E/4 (3.50mm) crochet hook

Yarn needle

SIZE AND FINISHED MEASUREMENTS

To fit: age 1(**3**:5) years; **chest** 20(**22**:24)in [51(**56**:61)cm]
Actual measurements after washing: chest 29(**32**:34½)in [74(**81**:87.5)cm];
length 15(**17**:18¼)in [38.5(**43.5**:46.5)cm];
sleeve (with cuff turned back) 7½(**9½**:11¼)in [19.5(**24**:29)cm]
Figures in parentheses refer to larger sizes. One figure refers to all sizes.

GAUGE

18 sts and 12 rows to 4in (10cm) over half double crochet, before washing, using E/4 (3.50mm) hook. Change hook size if necessary to obtain this gauge.

ABBREVIATIONS

ch = chain; **cont** = continue; **dec** = decrease; **hdc** = half double crochet; **2hdctog** = [yoh, insert hook in next st and pull loop through] twice, yoh and pull through all loops on hook; **3hdctog** = [yoh, insert hook in next st and pull loop through] 3 times, yoh and pull through all loops on hook; **RS** = right side; **sc** = single crochet; **st(s)** = stitch(es); **WS** = wrong side; **yoh** = yarn over hook; **[ ]** = work instructions in brackets as directed.

TIPS

▓ Do not count the 2 chain at the start of a row as a stitch.

▓ Work the starting chain loosely. If necessary, use a larger hook.

▓ Do not join in a new ball of yarn within a row or at the front edges; always join at a side edge so the ends can be woven into the seam.

▓ Don't weave in ends before washing the garment; use the shrunk yarn to sew up.

▓ Because indigo is a surface dye, the center of the yarn frays into little white tassels at the ends when washed, so tie a tight knot right at the end of each yarn end, then fold the yarn over and tie in a loose slip knot to keep it out of the way while the garment is washed.

▓ Tack the fronts together before washing.

▓ Although the ball band recommends hand washing, you can wash the duffel coat in a machine; just use a gentle wash action and make sure that the water temperature matches that given on the ball band. To preserve the color on subsequent washings, turn the coat inside out.

▓ You could make your own ring and toggle fastenings from brass curtain rings and wood, plastic, or horn toggles, or you could use traditional toggles and loops.

▓ You could use leather, cotton cord, or braid instead of narrow suede for the fastenings.

BACK

Make 69(**75**:81)ch.

Row 1 (WS) 1hdc in 3rd ch from hook, [1hdc in each ch] to end. *(67(**73**:79) sts.)*

Row 2 2ch, [1hdc in each hdc] to end. Row 2 forms hdc. Cont in hdc, work 47(**53**:57) more rows. Fasten off.

LEFT FRONT

Make 40(**43**:46)ch.

Row 1 (WS) Work as given for Row 1 of back. *(38(**41**:44) sts.)*

Cont in hdc as given for back, work 42(**46**:48) more rows **.

Shape neck. Next row (RS) 2ch, 1hdc in each of next 21(**24**:27)hdc, 3hdctog, 1hdc in next hdc, turn, leave 13hdc. *(23(**26**:29) sts.)* Mark 6th st from front edge. Work 1 row.

Dec row (RS) 2ch, [1hdc in each hdc] to last 4hdc, 3hdctog, 1hdc in last hdc. Cont in hdc, dec in this way at end of next 1(**2**:3) RS rows. *(19(**20**:21) sts.)* Work 1 row. Fasten off.

RIGHT FRONT

Work as left front to **. Fasten off.

Shape neck. Next row (RS) Leave 13hdc, join yarn in next hdc, 2ch, 1hdc in same hdc as join, 3hdctog, [1hdc in each hdc] to end. *(23(**26**:29) sts.)* Mark 6th st from front edge. Work 1 row.

Dec row (RS) 2ch, 1hdc in first hdc, 3hdctog, [1hdc in each hdc] to end. Cont in hdc, dec in this way at beg of next 1(**2**:3) RS rows. *(19(**20**:21) sts.)* Work 1 row. Fasten off.

SLEEVES

Make 36(**38**:42)ch.

Row 1 (WS) Work as given for Row 1 of back. *(34(**36**:40) sts.)*

Cont in hdc as back, work 5(**5**:7) rows.

Inc row 2ch, 1hdc in first hdc, 2hdc in next hdc, [1hdc in each hdc] to last 2hdc, 2hdc in next hdc, 1hdc in last hdc. Cont in hdc, inc in this way at each end of 6(**8**:9) foll 3rd rows. *(48(**54**:60) sts.)*

Work 3(**3**:4) rows. Fasten off.

HOOD

With WS together and fronts facing, join shoulders with a row of sc. Fasten off.

Make 93(**103**:113)ch.

Row 1 (WS) Work as given for Row 1 of back. *(91(**101**:111) sts.)*

Cont in hdc as back, work 2 rows.

Dec row (RS) 2ch, 2hdctog, [1hdc in each hdc] to last 2 hdc, 2hdctog. Cont in hdc, dec in this way at each end of next 4(**5**:6) RS rows. *(81(**89**:97) sts.)*

Work 5 rows.

1st side of back. Next row (RS) 2ch, 1hdc in each of next 30(**32**:34)hdc, turn. Cont in hdc until hood reaches from markers to center back neck. Fasten off.

2nd side of back With RS facing, leave center 21(**25**:29)hdc, join yarn in next hdc.

Next row 2ch, 1hdc in same place as join, [1hdc in each hdc] to end. *(30(**32**:34) sts.)* Complete to match first side. Fasten off.

POCKETS

(Make 2)

Make 16(**18**:20)ch. Work Row 1 as given for back. *(14(**16**:18) sts.)*

Cont in hdc as back, work 8(**9**:10) rows. Work 1 row crab st. Fasten off.

TO FINISH

With WS together and fronts facing, join back seam of hood with sc, then join row ends to sts left free at top of hood. Pin center back seam of hood to center back neck. Pin hood edge at intervals around neck edge between markers, easing to fit; join with sc. Work crab stitch along each front edge from hem to hood. Place markers 5¼ (**6**:6¾)in [13.5(**15**:17)cm] down from shoulders on back and fronts. Join sleeves between markers with sc. Sew on pockets. Wash and dry duffel. Sew side and sleeve seams, reversing seam at cuff for 1in (2.5cm). Turn back cuffs. Weave in ends. Cut the narrow suede into 8 equal lengths, loop through rings and thread through toggles, knot ends; sew on fronts.

Chapter 5
Equipment & Techniques

Equipment

All crochet stitches are based on the simple action of making loops
in a thread with a hook, but although the action is simple, the effects
achieved can vary enormously, from a delicate lacy look to a densely
textured fabric. If you've never tried crochet before, use a smooth,
medium-weight, light-colored yarn and a medium-size hook to
try out the basic stitches before starting a project.

Yarns

Wool, cotton, luxury fibers, and man-made fiber mixes in
a variety of weights can all be used for crochet. Although
smooth, firmly twisted yarns are the classic choice—because
the stitches can be seen clearly—interesting effects can be
created with the simplest of stitches in textured yarns.

Each project gives details of either the specific or generic
yarn type that was used to create the original item. Wherever
possible, stick with the recommended yarn, because this will
give you the effect shown in the picture. If you have to find a
substitute yarn, use the information about fiber content and
meterage given with each set of instructions to match

the original yarn as closely as possible. If you want to
try out one of the designs in an entirely different yarn,
the best thing to do is to crochet a sample with just
one ball to make sure you're happy with the result before
buying a quantity of yarn. As for the amount to buy, be
aware that this may be different, depending on the fiber
type and yarn construction. For example, even though
both yarns are described as a light worsted (DK), a
design worked in cotton will need more yarn than the
same item worked in 100% acrylic because cotton
is a heavier fiber.

Hooks

Depending on the size, crochet hooks can be made from
steel, aluminum, bamboo, plastic, or wood. Whichever you
choose, it's essential that the point and notch at the hook
end be smooth. If you are going to use the hook for
a lengthy project, choose a handle or a flattened grip
instead of a completely round shaft for comfort.

The instructions for each project give
a recommended hook size. This is the size
that was used to create the original
item. However, you may need to
use a different hook size
to obtain the correct
gauge (see page 113),
so it's always a good
idea to buy larger and
smaller hooks as well
as the stated size.

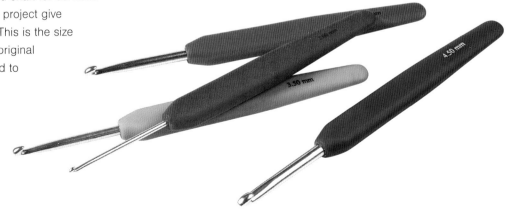

Additional equipment

Other items you'll need in order to make the projects in this book are a tape measure to check your gauge, a blunt-pointed sewing needle or tapestry needle to weave in ends, scissors for snipping yarn, markers to keep track of shaping rows, and blunt-pointed or long quilting pins to hold pieces in place while joining seams.

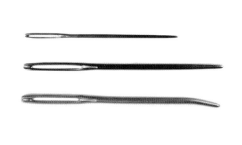

Following the instructions

Finished measurements

Each set of instructions provides the item's size in centimeters, using the yarn and hook size stated at the gauge given. Measurements in inches are also given in brackets. The designs were created in metric measurements, so the imperial measurements given are the closest equivalent. For garments, where appropriate, larger sizes are given in parentheses with colons between the figures. The "to fit" sizes are given as a guide for which size to make, but check that you will be happy with the finished actual measurements, because the amount of movement room varies according to the design. If in doubt, compare the actual measurements with a garment you already have at home.

Yarn

The yarn amounts given are based on the quantity of yarn used to make the original item. Although the hook size given is that used for the project, it is intended as a guide only. Always change the hook size and try again if you do not achieve the gauge given (see page 113).

Gauge

Gauge in crochet can vary enormously, probably because the stitch size is governed not just by the size of the hook but also by the way your fingers tension the yarn. Some of the projects in this book are so simple that you may feel that you can just dive in. But if your gauge is not correct, your time and the cost of the yarn could be wasted. See page 113 for how to make a swatch to check your gauge before you start a project.

Brackets

Instructions in square brackets should be repeated as indicated. Brackets are also used to clarify working a group of stitches. One or more asterisks are used to indicate a repeat or a part of the instructions to work again.

Techniques

In this section, you'll find all the simple crochet and finishing techniques that you'll need to make the projects in this book.

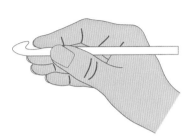

Holding the hook

Pick up your hook as though you are picking up a pen or pencil. Keeping the hook held between your fingers and thumb, turn your hand so that the palm is facing up and the hook is balanced in your hand and resting in the space between your index finger and your thumb.

You can also hold the hook like a knife—this may be easier if you are working with a large hook or with chunky yarn. Choose the method that you find most comfortable.

Holding the yarn

1 Pick up the yarn with your little finger in the opposite hand to your hook, with your palm facing upward and with the short end in front. Turn your hand to face downward, with the yarn on top of your index finger and under the other two fingers and wrapped right around the little finger, as shown above.

2 Turn your hand to face you, ready to hold the work in your middle finger and thumb. Keeping your index finger only at a slight curve, hold the work or the slip knot using the same hand, between your middle finger and your thumb and just below the crochet hook and loop/s on the hook.

Holding the hook and yarn while crocheting

Keep your index finger, with the yarn draped over it, at a slight curve, and hold your work (or the slip knot) using the same hand, between your middle finger and your thumb and just below the crochet hook and loop/s on the hook.

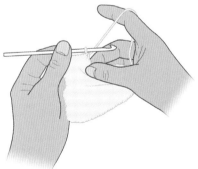

As you draw the loop through the hook release the yarn on the index finger to allow the loop to stay loose on the hook. If you tense your index finger, the yarn will become too tight and pull the loop on the hook too tight for you to draw the yarn through.

Holding the hook and yarn for left-handers

Some left-handers learn to crochet like right-handers, but others learn with everything reversed—with the hook in the left hand and the yarn in the right.

Making a slip knot

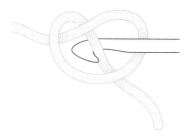

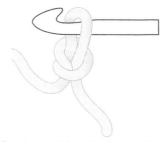

1 In one hand hold the circle at the top where the yarn crosses, and let the tail drop down at the back so that it falls across the center of the loop. With your free hand or the tip of a crochet hook, pull a loop through the circle.

2 Put the hook into the loop and pull gently so that it forms a loose loop on the hook.

Yarn over hook

To create a stitch, catch the yarn from behind with the hook pointing upward. As you gently pull the yarn through the loop on the hook, turn the hook so it faces downward and slide the yarn through the loop. The loop on the hook should be kept loose enough for the hook to slide through easily.

Magic ring

This is a useful starting technique if you do not want a visible hole in the center of your round. Loop the yarn around your finger, insert the hook through the ring, yarn over hook, pull through the ring to make the first chain. Work the number of stitches required into the ring and then pull the end to tighten the center ring and close the hole.

Chain

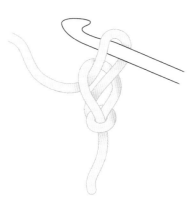

1 Using the hook, wrap the yarn over the hook ready to pull it through the loop on the hook.

2 Pull through, creating a new loop on the hook. Continue in this way to create a chain of the required length.

Chain ring

If you are crocheting a round shape, one way of starting off is by crocheting a number of chains following the instructions in your pattern, and then joining them into a circle.

1 To join the chain into a circle, insert the crochet hook into the first chain that you made (not into the slip knot), yarn over hook.

2 Pull the yarn through the chain and through the loop on your hook at the same time, thereby creating a slip stitch and forming a circle. You now have a chain ring ready to work stitches into as instructed in the pattern.

Chain space (ch sp)

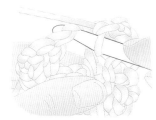

1 A chain space is the space that has been made under a chain in the previous round or row, and falls in between other stitches.

2 Stitches into a chain space are made directly into the hole created under the chain and not into the chain stitches themselves.

Slip stitch (sl st)

A slip stitch doesn't create any height and is often used as the last stitch to create a smooth and even round or row.

1 To make a slip stitch: first put the hook through the work, yarn round hook.

2 Pull the yarn through both the work and through the loop on the hook at the same time, so you will have 1 loop on the hook.

Making rounds

When working in rounds the work is not turned, so you are always working from one side. Depending on the pattern you are working, a "round" can be square. Start each round by making one or more chains to create the height you need for the stitch you are working:

Single crochet = 1 chain
Half double crochet = 2 chains
Double crochet = 3 chains
Treble crochet = 4 chains
Double treble crochet = 5 chains

Work the required stitches to complete the round. At the end of the round, slip stitch into the top of the chain to close the round.

Making rows

When making straight rows you turn the work at the end of each row and make a turning chain to create the height you need for the stitch you are working with, as for making rounds.

Single crochet = 1 chain
Half double crochet = 2 chains
Double crochet = 3 chains
Treble crochet = 4 chains
Double treble crochet = 5 chains

Working into top of stitch

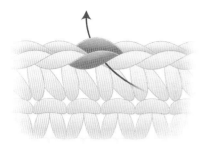

Unless otherwise directed, always insert the hook under both of the two loops on top of the stitch—this is the standard technique.

Working into front loop of stitch (FLO)

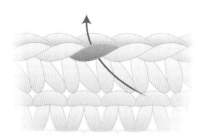

To work into the front loop of a stitch, pick up the front loop from underneath at the front of the work.

Working into back loop of stitch (BLO)

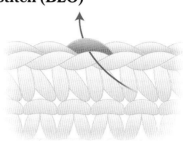

To work into the back loop of the stitch, insert the hook between the front and the back loop, picking up the back loop from the front of the work.

How to measure a gauge square

Using the hook and the yarn recommended in the pattern, make a number of chains to measure approximately 6in (15cm). Working in the stitch pattern given for the gauge measurements, work enough rows to form a square. Fasten off.

Take a ruler, place it horizontally across the square and, using pins, mark a 4in (10cm) area. Repeat vertically to form a 4in (10cm) square on the fabric. Count the number of stitches across, and the number of rows within the square, and compare against the gauge given in the pattern.

If your numbers match the pattern then use this size hook and yarn for your project. If you have more stitches, then your gauge is tighter than recommended and you need to use a larger hook. If you have fewer stitches, then your gauge is looser and you will need a smaller hook.

Make gauge squares using different size hooks until you have matched the gauge in the pattern, and use this hook to make the project.

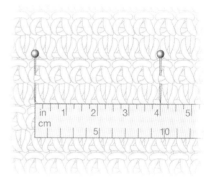

Single crochet (sc)

1 Insert the hook into your work, yarn over hook and pull the yarn through the work only. You will then have 2 loops on the hook.

2 Yarn over hook again and pull through the two loops on the hook. You will then have 1 loop on the hook.

Half double crochet (hdc)

1 Before inserting the hook into the work, wrap the yarn over the hook and put the hook through the work with the yarn wrapped around.

2 Yarn over hook again and pull through the first loop on the hook. You now have 3 loops on the hook.

3 Yarn over hook and pull the yarn through all 3 loops. You will be left with 1 loop on the hook.

Double crochet (dc)

1 Before inserting the hook into the work, wrap the yarn over the hook. Put the hook through the work with the yarn wrapped around, yarn over hook again and pull through the first loop on the hook. You now have 3 loops on the hook.

2 Yarn over hook again, pull the yarn through the first 2 loops on the hook. You now have 2 loops on the hook.

3 Pull the yarn through 2 loops again. You will be left with 1 loop on the hook.

Treble crochet (tr)

Yarn over hook twice, insert the hook into the stitch, yarn over hook, pull a loop through (4 loops on hook), yarn over hook, pull the yarn through 2 stitches (3 loops on hook), yarn over hook, pull a loop through the next 2 stitches (2 loops on hook), yarn over hook, pull a loop through the last 2 stitches. You will be left with 1 loop on the hook.

Double treble crochet (dtr)

Double trebles are "tall" stitches and are an extension on the basic double crochet stitch. They need a turning chain of 5 chains.

1 Yarn over hook three times, insert the hook into the stitch or space. Yarn over hook, pull the yarn through the work (5 loops on hook).

2 Yarn over hook, pull the yarn through the first 2 loops on the hook (4 loops on hook).

3 Yarn over hook, pull the yarn through the first 2 loops on the hook (3 loops on hook).

4 Yarn over hook, pull the yarn through the first 2 loops on the hook (2 loops on hook). Yarn over hook, pull the yarn through the 2 loops on the hook. You will be left with 1 loop on the hook.

Grouping stitches

Increase, fan, or shell

Working two or more complete stitches into the same stitch can be a method of increasing to shape a fabric, part of a decorative stitch pattern or an edging. Any stitch can be used, and the number of stitches worked varies. In this example three double crochet stitches are worked into one double crochet in the row below.

Make two or three stitches into one stitch or space from the previous row. The stitches are held together at the bottom but not at the top, making a fan shape.

Decrease or cluster

Working two or more partial stitches and taking them together at the top to make one stitch gives a decrease when working a fabric or a cluster in a stitch pattern. The basic technique for crocheting stitches together is the same, no matter which stitch you are using. The following example shows sc2tog.

Single crochet two stitches together (sc2tog)

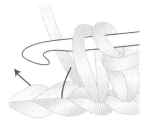

1 Insert the hook into your work, yarn over hook and pull the yarn through the work (2 loops on hook). Insert the hook in next stitch, yarn over hook and pull the yarn through.

2 Yarn over hook again and pull through all 3 loops on the hook. You will then have 1 loop on the hook.

Bobble

Bobbles are created when working on wrong-side rows and the bobble is then pushed out toward the right-side row. This is a four-double crochet cluster bobble (4dcCL).

1 Yarn over hook and then insert the hook in the stitch, yarn over hook and pull the yarn through the work.

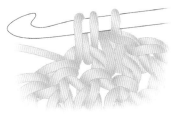

2 Yarn over hook and pull the yarn through the first 2 loops on the hook (2 loops on hook).

3 Repeat steps 1 and 2 three more times in the same stitch, yarn over hook and pull through all 5 loops on the hook.

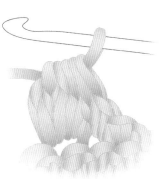

4 You can also make 1 chain to complete the bobble.

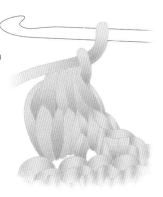

Popcorn

A popcorn differs from a cluster in that it is made up of complete stitches that are joined at the top. This example shows a popcorn made with four double crochet stitches worked into a foundation chain, but a popcorn can be worked into any stitch or space and can be made up of any practical number or combination of stitches.

1 Inserting the hook in the same place each time, work 4 complete double crochets.

2 Slip the hook out of the last loop and insert it into the top of the first stitch.

3 Then insert the hook into the loop of the last stitch again. Yarn over hook and pull it through as indicated.

4 This makes one complete popcorn.

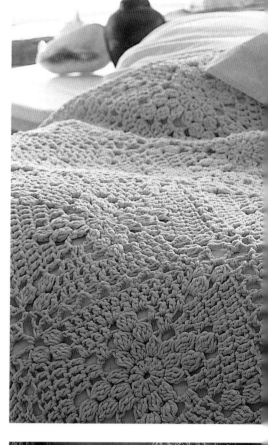

Joining yarn at the end of a row or round

You can use this technique when changing color, or when joining in a new ball of yarn as one runs out.

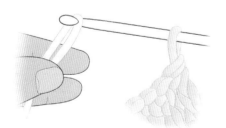

1 Keep the loop of the old yarn on the hook. Drop the tail and catch a loop of the strand of the new yarn with the crochet hook.

2 Draw the new yarn through the loop on the hook, keeping the old loop drawn tight and continue as instructed in the pattern.

Joining in new yarn after fastening off

You can use this technique when changing color, or when joining in a new ball of yarn as one runs out.

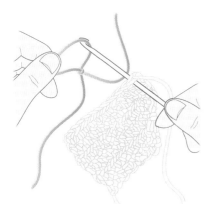 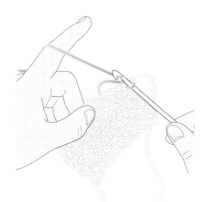

1 Fasten off the old color (see below). Make a slip knot with the new color (see page 111). Insert the hook into the stitch at the beginning of the next row, then through the slip knot.

2 Draw the loop of the slip knot through to the front of the work. Carry on working using the new color, following the instructions in the pattern.

Enclosing a yarn tail

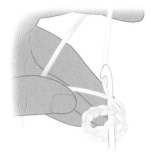

You may find that the yarn tail gets in the way as you work; you can enclose this into the stitches as you go by placing the tail at the back as you wrap the yarn. This also saves having to sew this tail end in later.

Fastening off

When you have finished crocheting, you need to fasten off the stitches to stop all your work unravelling.

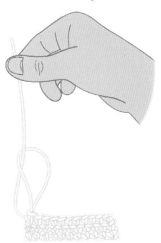

1 Draw up the final loop of the last stitch to make it bigger. Cut the yarn, leaving a tail of approximately 4in (10cm)—unless a longer end is needed for sewing up. Pull the tail all the way through the loop and pull the loop up tightly.

Weaving in yarn ends

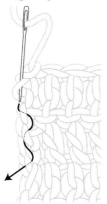

It is important to weave in the tail ends of the yarn so that they are secure and your crochet won't unravel. Thread a yarn needle with the tail end of yarn. On the wrong side, take the needle through the crochet one stitch down on the edge, then take it through the stitches, working in a gentle zig-zag. Work through four or five stitches then return in the opposite direction. Remove the needle, pull the crochet gently to stretch it and trim the end.

Blocking

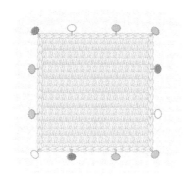

Crochet can tend to curl, so to make flat pieces stay flat you may need to block them. Pin the piece out to the correct size and shape on an ironing board, then cover with a cloth and press or steam gently (depending on the type of yarn—always follow the care instructions for the yarn you are using). Allow to dry completely before unpinning and removing from the board.

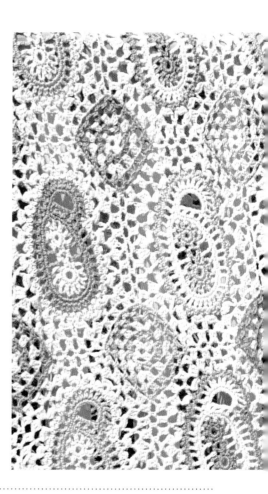

Surface chain

Surface crochet is a simple way to add extra decoration to a finished item, working slip stitches over the surface of the fabric.

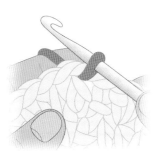

1 Using a contrast yarn, make a slip knot (see page 111). Holding the yarn with the slip knot behind the work and the hook in front, insert the hook between two stitches from front to the back and catch the slip knot behind the work with the hook. Draw the slip knot back through, so there is 1 loop on the hook at the front of the work.

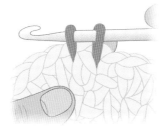

2 Insert the hook between the next 2 stitches, yarn over hook and draw a loop through to the front. You will now have 2 loops on the hook.

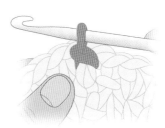

3 Pull the first loop on the hook through the second loop to complete the first slip stitch on the surface of the work. Repeat steps 2 and 3 to make the next slip stitch. To join two ends with an invisible join, cut the yarn and thread on to a yarn needle. Insert the needle up through the last stitch, into the first stitch as if you were crocheting it, then into the back loop of the previous stitch. Fasten off on the wrong side.

Crab stitch

This is simply single crochet worked backward to give a twisted edge. Crab stitch spreads the edge slightly, so there's no need to crease to turn a corner. If a straight edge flutes, either miss the occasional stitch or use a smaller hook.

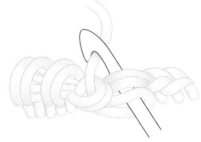

Do not turn the work at the end of the last row. Insert the hook in the last stitch to the right, yarn over hook, and pull through to make two loops twisted on the hook. Yarn over hook again and pull through making one loop on the hook. Repeat in the stitches along the edge or in row ends if necessary.

Single crochet seam

With a single crochet seam you join two pieces together using a crochet hook and working a single crochet stitch through both pieces, instead of sewing them together with a tail of yarn and a yarn sewing needle. This makes a quick and strong seam and gives a slightly raised finish to the edging. For a less raised seam, follow the same basic technique, but work each stitch in slip stitch rather than single crochet.

1 Start by lining up the two pieces with wrong sides together. Insert the hook in the top 2 loops of the stitch of the first piece, then into the corresponding stitch on the second piece.

2 Complete the single crochet stitch as normal and continue on the next stitches as directed in the pattern. This gives a raised effect if the single crochet stitches are made on the right side of the work.

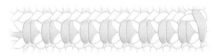

3 You can work with the wrong side of the work facing (with the pieces right side facing) if you don't want this effect and it still creates a good strong join.

Making an oversewn seam

An oversewn join gives a nice flat seam and is the simplest and most common joining technique.

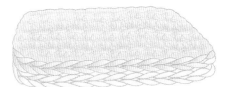
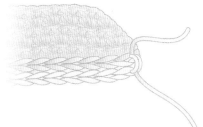
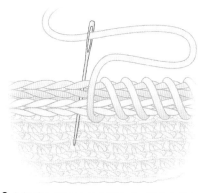

1 Thread a yarn sewing needle with the yarn you're using in the project. Place the pieces to be joined with right sides together.

2 Insert the needle in one corner in the top loops of the stitches of both pieces and pull up the yarn, leaving a tail of about 2in (5cm). Go into the same place with the needle and pull up the yarn again; repeat two or three times to secure the yarn at the start of the seam.

3 Join the pieces together by taking the needle through the loops at the top of corresponding stitches on each piece to the end. Fasten off the yarn at the end, as in step 2.

Mattress stitch seam

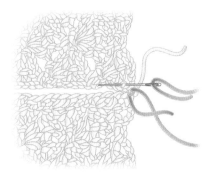

1 Line up the two pieces—pin them together if it helps make them more secure. Thread a tail of yarn in the same color as the pieces you're joining into a yarn sewing needle. Pick up a loop on the other side with the yarn sewing needle at a horizontal angle (90 degree angle) to the pattern and draw the yarn through loosely.

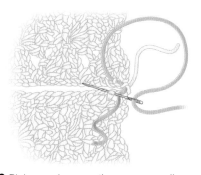

2 Pick up a loop on the corresponding side of the other piece just inside the edge and draw through the yarn. Leave the loops loose and don't draw them through tightly.

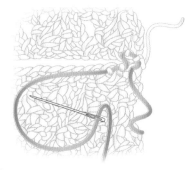

3 Pick up the next loop approx ⅜in (1cm) along on the same side and draw through the yarn.

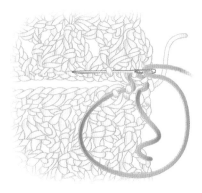

4 Pick up a loop on the corresponding side of the other piece just inside the edge and draw through the yarn. Leave the loops loose and don't draw them through tightly.

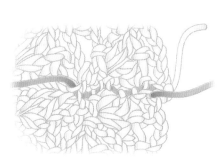

5 Repeat steps 3 and 4. When you have about 6 loops, hold the pieces firmly in place and pull the thread to draw the loose loops and bind the edging together.

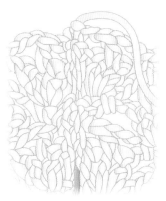

6 Continue in this way, repeating steps 3, 4, and 5 until the seam is joined. This will create an invisible seam on the right side of the work.

Pompom made with card circles

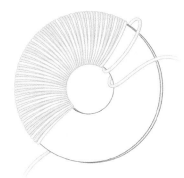 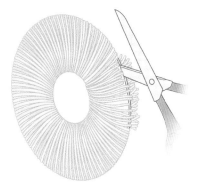

1 Using a pair of card rings cut to the size pompom you would like to create, cut a length of yarn and wind it around the rings until the hole in the center is filled.

2 Cut through the loops around the outer edge of the rings and ease slightly apart. Thread a length of yarn between the layers and tie tightly, leaving a long end. Remove the card rings and fluff up the pompom. The long yarn tail can be used to sew the pompom in place.

Care of crochet items

Store crocheted garments folded flat. If you put them on a hanger, they will droop. Follow the recommended wash code for the yarn as given on the ball band. If in doubt, hand wash and dry flat, at least for the first time, so you can monitor the result. If using a washing machine, treat any stains, then turn the garment inside out before washing and reshape it while it is still damp.

Crochet stitch conversion chart

Crochet stitches are worked in the same way in both the USA and the UK, but the stitch names are not the same and identical names are used for different stitches. Below is a list of the US terms used in this book, and the equivalent UK terms.

USA TERM	UK TERM
single crochet (sc)	double crochet (dc)
half double crochet (hdc)	half treble (htr)
double crochet (dc)	treble (tr)
treble (tr)	double treble (dtr)
double treble (dtr)	triple treble (trtr)
gauge	tension
yarn over hook (yoh)	yarn round hook (yrh)

Suppliers

We cannot cover all stockists here, so please explore the local yarn stores and online retailers in your own country. If you wish to substitute a different yarn for the one recommended in the pattern, try the Yarnsub website for suggestions: www.yarnsub.com.

USA

Jo-Ann Fabric and Craft Stores
Yarns and craft supplies
www.joann.com

Knitting Fever Inc.
www.knittingfever.com

LoveCrafts
Online sales
www.lovecrafts.com

Michaels
Craft supplies
www.michaels.com

WEBS
www.yarn.com

UK

Hobbycraft
Yarn and craft supplies
www.hobbycraft.co.uk

John Lewis
Yarn and craft supplies
Telephone numbers of
stores on website
www.johnlewis.com

Laughing Hens
Online sales
Tel: +44 (0) 1829 740903
www.laughinghens.com

LoveCrafts
Online sales
www.lovecrafts.com

Wool
Yarn, hooks
Store in Bath.
+44 (0)1225 469144
www.woolbath.co.uk

Wool Warehouse
Online sales
www.woolwarehouse.co.uk

Australia

Black Sheep Wool 'n' Wares
Retail store and online
Tel: +61 (0)2 6779 1196
www.blacksheepwool.com.au

Index

Acknowledgments

I would like to thank everyone who helped me with this book, especially Cindy Richards for giving me the opportunity to work on this project and for her support, taste, and enthusiasm. Thanks also to Liz Dean for her calm guidance and editing; without you Liz, I may never have finished!

Thanks to Debbie Bliss and all at Designer Yarns, Mike Cole and all at Elle, Kate Buller and all at Rowan, and David Rawson, Caroline Powell, and all at Sirdar for the inspirational yarns.

For help with turning ideas into reality, thank you to Betty Speller for the Textured Cardigan Coat and to Lesley Stanfield for the Lacy Victorian Shawl. Many thanks to Tino Tedaldi for the lovely photographs, Sue Rowlands for the styling, and especially to Sally Powell for her care in bringing the visuals together. Thanks to Roger Hammond for designing the book. Thanks to the models: Francoise Wolff, Simona Busimuco, Eleanor Reilly, Amit Dhaliwal, Louise MacSweeney, Daisy MacSweeney, and Silvia Arganda and baby.

Finally a huge thank you to Sue Horan for her excellent, patient, and through checking of my instructions.

I would like to dedicate this book to my mother, Hilda Griffiths, in memory of her life 19th July 1917 to 6th November 2006.